Generation Gap

Liz & Anna Hinds

First published in 1999 by
KEVIN MAYHEW LTD
Buxhall
Stowmarket
Suffolk IP14 3BW

© 1999 Liz and Anna Hinds

The right of Liz and Anna Hinds to be identified as the authors of this work has been asserted by them in accordance with the Copyright, Designs and Patents Act 1988.

All rights reserved. No part of this publication may be reproduced, stored in a retrieval system, or transmitted, in any form or by any means, electronic, mechanical, photocopying, recording or otherwise, without the prior written permission of the publisher.

0 1 2 3 4 5 6 7 8 9

ISBN 1 84003 441 6
Catalogue No 1500308

Cover design by Jonathan Stroulger
Edited by Elisabeth Bates
Printed and bound in Great Britain

Contents

Acknowledgements 5
Introduction 7

Life without her 8

1995
Letters from the trenches 10
Independence Day 12
It's good to talk 14

1996
The Clothes Show 16
Saturday Night Fever 18
Sea, sand 'n' sun, sun, sun 20

1997
Our **V**ery **W**onderful baby 22
Putting the 'L' in life 24
Shop 'till you drop 26
The best days of your life? 28

1998
Fever pitch 30
En vacances (Postcard from France) 32
R-Letter Day 34
Good job hunting 36
Man about the house 39
Lurve 42
'In heaven an angel is nobody in particular' 44
The demon drink 46
Ambrosia 49
The only way is up 52
Random jottings 54
The sounds of music 56
Boyfriends 59
The big sleep 62

Acknowledgements

Anna's

Pop, Rob, Neil and Harvey . . . for being bald, annoying, loud, cute and inspiring (collectively).
Mum . . . who didn't do as much work as me this time, and for being my mum and friend!
Steve . . . for learning, and letting me shave his head.
The house . . . for being my eternal safe place.
Katie, Laa-Laa, Danette and Suzanne . . . who helped shape the me I am today, during the four-year writing of this book!

Liz's

Mine are much simpler! Mike, Rob and Neil because you put up with a scruffy home and late meals in the name of creativity, and Anna, because you always encourage and, anyway, this book would not have been possible without you! Also to Jill Worth who gave us our first break and Dave Gatward who gave us our second.

Introduction

Anna's Introduction

We've had fights over the years. Fights full of tears, and sulking, and tantrums, and shouting, and all the weapons that teenage angst can call to its aid. Fights over clothes; hair colour; food; being driven around. Really, fights over everything that I wanted and couldn't have.

And now, I can reflect on it all and think how much I've matured, and stopped kicking and screaming ... er ... OK, OK, I hate to deceive you. After all, we are about to let you into what were the most private, and embarrassing times of our lives ... well, my life, at least. We are about to strip off all our protective garments, in front of your very eyes, and reveal each other – from adolescence to adulthood, from naïve mother to weary woman. What you see here is the unashamed, unhidden, naked and blushing daughter and mother – access all areas.

I think I need to go and lie down before you read any further.

Liz's PS

We started writing these articles in 1995 when Anna was 15 and I was forty-something. The earlier ones originally appeared in a church newspaper and then *Parentwise* magazine. The idea was that we chose a subject, such as nose-piercing or nightclubbing, and wrote about it, each from our own perspective. We didn't get to see what the other had written until we had both finished and then we weren't allowed to change anything. On some topics we disagree big time, while on others our views are remarkably similar.

But you see, in the end, 'As is the mother, so is her daughter.' Ezekiel 16:44

Life without her

The mother's view

I've always thought that one benefit of having children was the fact that they would look after you or at least visit you when you're old. Now it transpires that Anna isn't going to put me in a home – she's going to keep me in the shed. Seeing the look on my face at this discovery she sought to reassure me. 'Don't worry, Mum, I'll pass cups of tea through the window to you.' Why do we bother? And wouldn't life be different without her . . . ?

It would be quiet for a start. No more unidentifiable music at full volume rending the air.

It would mean hassle-free evenings where we could relax without having to watch the clock for the moment we have to pick her up or take her somewhere.

It would mean cheaper phone bills and the ability to use the telephone when I want without waiting for the latest vital piece of information to be passed on.

It would be less stressful without the 'discussions' over whether she, as a fifteen year old, should be allowed to go to over-18 discos.

It would mean greater peace of mind without the worry over whether she'll get involved with drugs or pregnant or emotionally hurt.

And with all the money we'd save, we could have fabulous foreign holidays every year.

But who would put a surprise hot water bottle in my bed when husband's away? Who would share my love of the Beatles? Or my chocolate as we sit and watch Pride and Prejudice? Who would plait my hair for me? Who would read what I write and say encouraging things about it? Who would sigh and say 'Oh Mum' as I relate my latest disaster? And still love me?

My daughter, my friend. And I thank God for her.

The daughter's view

'Lock me in the SHED????' my mother shrieks. She is leaning on a worktop in the kitchen and her concern is provoked by an announcement I made a minute ago.

'We're not putting you in a home, mother . . .'

She smiled fondly, expecting a soppy declaration. I continued, 'Homes cost MONEY . . . and I don't want you nagging me for the rest of my life, so you can't live with me. So . . .'

'We'll put you in the shed,' Robert suggested.

'Lock you in the shed,' I corrected.

'I'll bash a hole in the wall with my walking stick, and shout to the milkman, and tell him to phone the National Society for The Prevention of Cruelty to ... mothers,' she threatened.

'Then we'll barricade the door.' *

My mother is now muttering to herself, grasping her cup of tea. And I watch, and I think: in a life without her, I wouldn't ever have to brew her tea again. And, I sigh, I wouldn't have to worry about money to put her in a home. Good grief, I think, I'm getting as bad as her, talking to myself.

And I'm still thinking about 'life without mother' as I fetch her slippers (the dog would, only he doesn't fully understand the 'man's best friend' bit yet) and find her a ripe banana and turn the TV over because she's 'comfy' and then listen to her guilt trip when I complain. And I start to wonder if life without her would be that bad after all ...

Then again. Who would I watch *Pride and Prejudice* with, without worrying about crying? My dad would have it turned off if she wasn't so insistent.

Who would call me down from my room when I'm listening to music, to take phone calls? I know she complains, but she struggles on, and my dad or brother would just hang up on my call if I didn't answer.

Who would I ask about the Beatles? Well, for long periods anyway. And who would stand around and listen to me when I need someone to listen, at eleven o'clock at night when I drag in, exhausted and down? Who would help me in my endless efforts to get a glimpse of the new neighbours, and who else would plot with me to cunningly 'lose' a ball in their garden?

Who would wake me up in the morning (especially with the fuss I put up)? Who would cook me my vegetarian meals when I'm just too tired to do it?

And as I flop down on the sofa next to my mother, and share some chocolate, and we switch on the weepy film taped from last night, and settle down for a peaceful cry, I do wonder where I would be without her.

*thought for the day:
'Rise in the presence of the aged, show respect for the elderly and revere your God.' Leviticus 19:32

'Let us not love with words or tongue, but with actions and in truth.'
1 John 3:18

1995: Letters from the trenches

The mother's view

A battle is being waged in our house. Quite separate from the everyday rucks and mauls, this is a war of subtlety where the main tactic is Wearing Down the Resistance.

The first blow was struck a couple of years ago, although at that stage I didn't realise it was a war. Anna wanted to have her ears pierced. I held out until I felt she was old enough to make such a decision and then quite happily accompanied her to the shop. In fact, I went one step further and had my own ears pierced as well!

So that was that, I thought. But I hadn't taken fashion into account. Next it was, 'Mum, can I have another earring in the top of my ear?' 'No, definitely not.'

I honestly can't remember agreeing to it or even when it happened. It must have been battle fatigue numbing the brain. Suffice it to say, Anna now has a second earring in one ear — not that you can see it under her hair anyway.

So one boundary has been exceeded and a new one created.

'Can I have my nose pierced?' 'Absolutely and positively NO!' The trouble is, I can't really think of a good reason why not. I only have the parent's favourite 'Because I say so' to fall back on. Which brings me to today's dilemma — to bleach or not to bleach? Anna has dark brown hair which she would love to transform to white. My gut reaction is that 'It'll ruin your hair and it will all fall out.' Of course, as I have no actual scientific backing I have to do a lot of waffling. I suspect a compromise is around the corner and that we will allow her to bleach some streaks before she sets off for Greenbelt, otherwise I fear that she might take it into her head to do it while there.

But now, of course, the cracks in Mum's armour have shown. It has been proved that I am quite likely to crumble under pressure. I've always tried to be consistent. If I said no I meant no. Surely I'm not so weak that I can be bullied by my children, not to mention the dog . . . or the cat?

Ah well, if all else fails, I'll have to call in the big guns . . . 'Michael'.

The daughter's view

'No!'

And so began the Bleach War.

Battles such as this, with my parents as the opposition, in the past have had a 50/50 success rate to either side. Admittedly, the Ear War in '93 (I wanted the top of one ear pierced) resulted in me being grounded when I won – they denied everything. That was my one proud win. However, in 1995, the tables turned and I lost (for now). I am not having my nose pierced on the grounds of 'I say so'; or at least not 'till I'm 18. I think they're hoping that I'm going to turn into a boring sensible person overnight on my 18th. But you see it's become principle now. Even if I do change my mind about having my nose pierced (and I haven't yet) clearly, they've left me with no choice.

And now we're into a new one. War III, thus smashing all world records. The chances on either side are equal . . .

The only reason I'm struggling on is that my parents have agreed to allow me to bleach streaks in my hair. What I'm hoping for is to bleach all of it. But I wouldn't leave it white; that would look horrible. I want to dye it pink on top, so it comes out really bright. I'm going to a music festival, Greenbelt, and I need to be outrageous for it. It'll be worth my hair falling out! (Which, by the way, is my parents' sole argument. My hair will fall out if I bleach it. Yeah . . . right. Personally I think they'll just be too embarrassed to have a daughter with pink hair.) I've found the dye and rung the hairdressers about the bleaching – there's only one problem to overcome.

The Other Side.

I tried the Mature Persuasive tactic, the calm, reasonable argument.

I used the Other Parents tactic (other-people-let-their-children-be-responsible-for-their-own-hair).

I even resorted to the sulky 'I'm doing it anyway' tactic, and the 'what will you do if I do it?' and even foot-stamping in order to get my way. All plans to stay calm have flown the nest by this stage, and all the early childhood methods have come back into play. You see I'm very organised really. If all else fails, cry.

> **Run away from the silly, pointless obsessions in your young head. Instead concentrate on searching for love, and making peace. Oh, and don't go looking for an argument, because you know that will only cause trouble.** 2 Timothy 2:22-23 (rephrased)

Independence Day

The mother's view

It all began innocently enough. A few years ago the local police started running alcohol-free discos for young teenagers and Anna was keen to join in this harmless fun. So one Tuesday evening you would have found me with my nose pressed to the window anxiously awaiting Cinderella's return from the ball. She had gone with a group of friends and was being brought home by another mum. Regular media reports of the rising crime rate do little to calm the nerves of parents and the thought of our first-born wandering the city centre late at night ... still, what harm could she possibly come to leaving the disco and getting into a car?

Just as I was on the point of phoning the police and the hospitals Anna strolled in. 'Sorry I'm late, but it wasn't my fault!' There followed a tale of everyone trying to leave at the same time, the resultant queue for coats and being the last person to be dropped off. An innocent story totally unlike the scenes of violence and mayhem which had been running through my brain for the longest half hour ever. And that was just one Tuesday from a lifetime. And just the start of my worries.

Becoming independent is, of course, a vital part of growing up. As parents we have to help, albeit with hearts in mouths, our offspring to prepare to leave the nest. But with independence comes responsibility. So if they're to go somewhere, we must be sure they will behave sensibly, even if others don't, and we must know how they're getting home.

Of course, now at sixteen, Anna is confident of her ability to cope with any situation and hurries off when I start on my 'Now don't take drinks off anyone etc.' routine. And the thought that, in just a year or so's time, my children could be in cars driven by seventeen-year-old boys is enough to ensure that I rush to get my car keys!

I could say that growing up is about putting your dirty clothes in the laundry basket instead of leaving them in a corner of the bedroom, about offering to help instead of grumbling when asked, about ignoring your little brother's jibes instead of hitting him, but I won't. I'll just say that as parents we are trying our best to help our children develop into independent adults. Sometimes we get it wrong. But it's all done because we love them.

The daughter's view

I think that I've always wanted to be independent. When I was about three, anytime the garden gate was left open, out I would be, like a crazed maniac, desperate for freedom. I would totter down the road as fast as I could. My parents found this hilarious. They came after me, every time, but only to snap photos for later amusement. We still have pictures of young Anna running down the street, cardigan flying out behind me. I still don't know what the neighbours thought. Probably that my parents were beating, starving or locking me up, from the speed I was going. One thing was going through my head: get out!

You might think, from this, that my parents don't love me. I know that they do (I do notice the many lectures on 'only wanting the best for you'). They don't starve or beat me; it's just that I have a desire to be independent. Maybe all teenagers go through it! That's what my dad would say. Typical teenage phase. I'll grow out of it. And I'll look back and see what a huge twit I was (in his phrasing). You see, everything I do and say is:

a) 'a load of rubbish'
b) 'typical teenage reaction or phase'.

Anyway, I have always wanted to be independent. I love being in the house on my own, I love being trusted with money, I love catching my own buses, I love being able to go out late, I love having my own money coming in (addressed to me, and me alone!).

I picture university as Anne Shirley (as in *Anne of Green Gables* fame) lived it; in a big shared house with loads of 'soulmate' housemates, taking it in turns to do the cooking, buying Oxfam clothes, keeping to a budget and eating rice every night! I know my ideas may be a bit dreamlike and all the people reading this who have been through it probably have very different memories. But I can dream, can't I? The best part is planning what to eat so my money doesn't run out, economising – having my own rooms that I can tidy when I feel like it, and making my own cups of tea! It's the actual not-having-to-rely-on-anybody-else bit that gets me. And of course the idea of eating chips every day has its appeal too . . .

> **God, you stand back, let us get on with it and make our own mistakes, then you pick up the pieces and put us back together again. It would be so much easier for you if we were just automatons, but you chose to give us free will and suffer the consequences. Help me to let go.**
>
> **You can't walk into the darkness on your own; what makes you think you can do it without God? You must hold hands and walk in the light, together; and God will be with you. 1 John 1:7 (rephrased)**

It's good to talk

The mother's view

Last year British Telecom made £111 profit per second. That's £6660 a minute, and that's profit remember. If, like me, you're the parent of a teenage girl, you won't be surprised, in fact you've probably already realised that you're contributing a large part of it.

I used to think it was a sitcom joke, girls rushing in from school and straightaway phoning their friends. Not any more. Our last itemised phone bill showed that over half the calls were made by Anna and those are just the more expensive ones which show up. It amazes me that girls can spend all day together in school and then find so much to say to each other just twenty minutes after separating.

What really aggravates me is when I enter the room and Anna's on the phone and she says, 'I can't talk now, my mother's just come in. Go away, Mum.' Is anything more likely to make a mother hover outside the door, ears on stalks, than that? – but I digress.

If you've seen the BT adverts on television you'll have realised that they're trying to ensnare more men into using the phone for 'friendly chats'. They probably spent millions of pounds on research to discover that women spend more time talking on the phone than men when I could have told them that for a fraction of the cost! In the past, my son's phone calls have typically gone like this: 'Hello Jon. It's Rob. Do you want to play football? ... OK, I'll meet you down the playing fields in half an hour. Bye.'

But now with a girlfriend on the scene all that's changed. Our latest phone bill has confirmed that, with a girl on the other end of the line, even the most tongue-tied of boys can run up a charge.

So what do we do about it? Threats to make Anna pay are pointless as she doesn't have that kind of money. Pleas to 'get off the phone now' are shushed and waved away. I suppose I could put my foot down ... and disconnect her.

Or perhaps I'll just write to BT and ask them to change their slogan so that smiling Bob Hoskins says 'It's good to talk ... but only if someone else is paying!'

The daughter's view

BT are dirty, cunning rats. They are crafty beyond measure; they have gone *out of their way* to make my life a misery. Why? Because, of course, they are the inventors of ... the parents' pet, the teen-trap. The *itemised phone bill*. I mean, of all the sneaky, low-down, cruel things to do. They have created the one thing which can catch us out. Goodbye lovely long evenings of luxurious hassle-free phoning! BT are now recording every phone call we make. Now, we are exposed.

So, I invented a foolproof plan. A plan which would enable me to make long anonymous phone calls which didn't show on the itemised bill! However, two little holes appeared in my clever scheme. One, my mother overheard me telling a friend about it, and two, nobody else in my house makes long phone calls. So when the next phone bill arrived (the sound of it falling through the letterbox is imprinted on my memory like my own funeral march), it was actually pretty brick-red obvious as to who the culprit was. 'LOOK AT THIS!' my father's voice boomed at me. I was still in morning-mode, i.e. asleep but hungry, and my father appeared as an angry blob in front of my glasses. So the news failed to make an impact and I passed him to pour my branflakes.

My father is constantly bringing up how much money I owe him, but I usually run away with my fingers in my ears; this is my favoured approach to most things involving money. Unless it is being given to me. I have, so far, escaped the bill.

Now I am 'being responsible' with the telephone. That means only ringing someone if I'm really bored, or if I haven't seen them for over 20 minutes, or over urgent matters like what to wear today. And naturally these 'short' calls escalate into something quite a lot longer. Perhaps it's programmed into our systems. Phonoholicism, a genetic addiction which draws and grips us so that we are physically unable to hang up the receiver . . . an addiction which sucks at your soul and takes every ounce of self-control to give up. Perhaps teenagers have a hormone inside them which gives sudden urges to lift that handset and dial those numbers, like a baby scrabbling for milk.

Why doesn't anyone else understand my relationship with the telephone? It's like the teenager's equivalent of a cup of tea, providing a cosy satisfaction and that warm happiness. Nobody needs the phone like I do.

PS. Dear Dad, Take Note:

> 'Jesus said, "Two men (children) owed money to a certain moneylender (phone bill payer). One owed him five hundred denarii (pounds) and the other fifty. Neither had the money to pay him back, so he cancelled the debts of both. Now which loves him more?"
> Simon replied, "The one who had the biggest debt cancelled."
> "You have judged correctly," said Jesus. "He who is forgiven more gives more love back."' Taken from Luke 7: 41-43

1996: The Clothes Show

The mother's view

'Do I look all right?'

'Yeah, okay.'

'What do you mean "okay"? What's wrong with it?'

One careless word can reduce my confident, arrogant even, sixteen year old to a mass of self doubts. Such is the insecurity of the teenage years. All appears calm on the surface but one small pebble dropped in breaks the tension holding that calm together and the ripples are felt to the very edges.

Other mothers, who have been through it already, assure me this is quite normal. I suppose it should come as no surprise. Life presses in on them from the outside and their hormones churn them up on the inside. Little wonder they are so vulnerable.

Actually I have no complaint about Anna's clothes. I can't really, as she's started wearing my old ones! (When I say 'old' I mean twenty-five years or so.) We were clearing out the attic recently when we came across an old dress of mine from the days of 'flower power'. Initially I put it to be thrown out but suddenly wondered if Anna would wear it. She would. She's also uncovered a baggy old cardigan which she drapes around herself.

They say there's nothing new in fashion – all clothes come back 'in' eventually. Although I think Anna would consider it an insult to be 'in'. She likes to think of herself as an individualist, not following the trends, more, what used to be called, a hippie. As I'm a leftover hippie myself, we get along quite well.

I'm happiest in jeans or long skirts but have started feeling I should dress my age more so my wardrobe now includes some shorter straight skirts. I'm trying but I haven't yet sussed getting in and out of cars elegantly. How these elegant women manage without flashing their knickers at the world beats me.

A few years ago we attended a coming of age party. The eighteen-year-old in question was a stunning blonde who wore a glamorous black frothy creation ... and Doc Martens. This regulation footwear is actually quite practical from both foot health and self defence angles. Okay, so it takes a bit of getting used to seeing your daughter in what appear, at first glance, to be army boots, but they're heaps better than stilettos!

The daughter's view

'What are you dressed up posh for?' I ask, hearing clicky heels crossing the hall.

'I'm going to deliver some work. I'm wearing my businesswoman clothes!'

Even in her 'businesswoman clothes', my mother looks far from posh. She has made an effort though: a skirt instead of the usual tatty trousers or jeans, and ladderless tights, and high heels. Oh, and her decent jumper (i.e. no rips). She looks awkward in her heels (they're new) and itching to get out of them. She sees my bemused face and tries to pretend that she's used to looking smart. She can't fool me though. So what you're getting is the truth behind the heels …

Her favourite shoes are trainers. And not your average trainers. Trainers with soil encrusted on them from the 1950s, with holes from when her feet were still growing, and worn soles which fit her feet to a millimetre. When I am forced to borrow them for PE, my friends get hysterical.

What else? Sweatshirts with more holes than fabric; jeans which 'Gap' would pay a fortune to fade like that.

But you're getting the wrong end of the stick. I am not ashamed of my mother's wardrobe, far, far from it. I am very proud that she wears jeans. She presents a far friendlier image like that. Shoulder-pads and floral prints and straight skirts do nothing for her. I'm going to dress exactly like she does when I reach her age.

When she was younger, too, it seems, she had good taste in clothes. Sitting here typing this now, I've just realised that I am in fact wearing not only a cool dress from my mother's youth, but also a selection of rings which were hers too. I have salvaged many of her bin-bound clothes – yesterday I made another delightful discovery which now hangs proudly in my own wardrobe. Our attic should be renamed Oxfam and opened for business.

Now, I'm supposed to write about my own clothes taste too. But being fickle, and changing my image constantly, from 'tramp' to 'hippie' to '70s chick', perhaps I should leave that to my mother, who will no doubt have plenty to say on it.

> Thank you, God, that in spite of what the world might tell us, what we wear doesn't make us. Give us a glimpse of what you see both in us and in others.

Saturday Night Fever

The mother's view

Anna is indignant. 'Other peoples' parents let them stay out 'till two and then get a taxi home.'

I remember a time when 'other peoples' parents' were a source of comfort to me. The daily chat at the school gate, when the children were young, provided reassurance that I was not alone in my concerns.

Now, however, my children are all in senior school. They have made new friends, many with both parents working, and no longer want to be met after school. (They still want to be picked up but heaven help me if I dare get out of the car to chat, thus bringing untold embarrassment on to them.) The resultant lack of parental communication has given the children the upper hand and they are able to manipulate to their hearts' content. I have come to hate the omnipotent entity that 'other peoples' parents' have become.

What started, for Anna, as an occasional visit to a police-run disco for young teens has developed into a fairly regular trip to the real world of over-eighteen clubs complete, no doubt, with sex and drugs and rock'n'roll.

When she first brought up the idea of visiting Cinderella's we were adamant. 'No, you're too young.' In response we were told that 'everyone from my class goes, and if I wait until I am eighteen, I'll be the oldest person there.' Eventually we agreed, initially as a birthday treat, on condition that we collected her at half past eleven. Gradually, of course, both the frequency of visits and the lateness of the hour at which she has to leave edged up. 'Nobody gets there until half past eleven and no-one leaves before half past one' allegedly.

Anna's friends' parents have all surrendered, leaving us the only ones who still refuse to let her get a taxi and insist on dragging her out early. (Of course what she views as early is way past the bedtime of old fogies like us, resulting in grumpiness all round.)

Still, as we crawl into bed at some unearthly hour, I can only thank God for answered prayer in her safe return.

The daughter's view

It's a tight schedule:
4:30: colour hair, shave legs and armpits. Cut legs several times
5:00: rinse hair, attempt to neaten and paint nails

5:30:	shower, wash hair
5:45:	dry, moisturise all over, dress, brush and set hair
6:00:	eat. Sit at table watched by parents until the last crumb is gone
6:30:	ring round checking arrangements
7:00:	fight furiously with olds for a later curfew
7:15:	watch *Blind Date* under the mistaken impression that there is plenty of time left
7:30:	panic – only fifteen minutes to picking-up. Start to slap make-up on
7:45:	dash around house searching for new mascara
7:50:	finish make-up at last
7:51:	friend rings to say lift will be late. Collapse into a chair, with nothing left to do, and feel convinced that there is.
8.30:	Arrive at destination, after four hours of preparation.

Yes, a tight schedule, which requires huge amounts of concentration and organisation. And for what? One night at a club, or less if my parents can possibly help it.

At first I had to be picked up at twelve. With cunning and helped along by their convenient memory loss, I managed to bump it up to twelve-thirty. The week after my exams, I had a glorious triumph with one-thirty (fluke, I think) but that was a one-off and now I'm easing them along to one. All you have to do is be mature, not have temper tantrums, and allow for the fact that old people need more sleep than I do. Teenagers are more alert in the night than any other time of day, says scientific research; but any good partying teenager could tell you that.

My parents would never believe it but everyone else can stay later than me. They can! And what do I say to a gorgeous bloke who wants to know why I can't stay for another drink? I'm terribly sorry but my mummy and daddy say I have to be in bed by one o'clock. Well goodbye reputation.

The sad fact is, I am forced to run out of the club early, jacket over my head, and jump in the car in a desperate bid to get away unseen. Does that sound fair to you?!

> 'If I go up to the heavens, you are there; if I make my bed in the depths, you are there. If I rise on the wings of the dawn, if I settle on the far side of the sea, even there your right hand will guide me, your right hand will hold me fast.' Psalm 139: 8-10

Sea, sand 'n' sun, sun, sun

The mother's view

'You're staying in a caravan?' My friend was amazed. As someone who spends weeks each year in foreign hotels she found it hard to believe that not only was I happy with a caravan, I was looking forward to it. Our annual break from routine.

Family holidays are not easy to arrange for a number of reasons. Each Spring we consult brochures full of white sands, blue sea and sun, sun, sun. Then we work out the cost and decide we don't really want to spend that much to be stuck in a lookalike apartment surrounded by lots of people being jolly. So we plump yet again for caravanning in this country and spend a week in a look-alike caravan surrounded by jolly people, the only differences being it rains and it costs more.

That's assuming we can squeeze a week into the children's hectic schedules. If it's not Scout camp, it's Greenbelt or church holidays, but eventually we manage it and off we set. Our attempts to spot the Beast of Bodmin are foiled by the fog and rain, but are we deterred? No, I think British weather is a bonus. The perils of lying in the sun have been imprinted on my brain and eroded any pleasure; I'm far too concerned about whether I've covered every visible bit of the children's skin to relax. Anyway, the best bit about holidays is the opportunity they provide to catch up on reading and that's just as easily done, and probably more comfortably done, in the caravan as on a hot sandy beach.

We might have had our last holiday as a family though. Anna and her friends have great plans for their hols after their A-levels finish. Find the cheapest possible apartment in Ibiza or Majorca and party through the night. Did I say I was worried about sunburn? Forget it, we are now in Major Worry League.

The hope I'm hanging on to is that she won't have saved enough money to do it. At every opportunity I'm encouraging her to spend, spend, spend.

But suppose she goes? Even if I was on the same island, I'd never be allowed to go to the clubs and discos with her. She would still be out of my reach. Thank God she won't be alone though; she'll have someone closer than a mother with her.

The daughter's view

'Right. Tomorrow morning I'll get up at ten, do twenty laps of the pool, do my shopping, come back to the caravan, two hours of homework, and off to town for the evening.' Well, it's eleven o'clock and I've just been woken up by the dog and brothers bashing the wall between my head and the, um, 'kitchen'. Let me explain to any virgin caravanners. It's not a wall, more like a sheet, through which

I can hear every breath, every crunch and every step of my family. I've just gotten used to it – I sleep heavily – only now they've discovered that they can wake me up by sending the dog up and down the corridor outside, and bashing his tail against what is actually my face. Mother and Father are up, in fact they've already been out for milk, and are sickeningly bright and cheerful. My holiday time is late at night, whereas my family's is first thing in the morning.

It's hard enough being in an enclosed space with them all for a week, but it gets worse – the days are full of 'fun' things like 'family' crazy golf. Although, my friend (I've dragged her along to avoid death-by-boredom) and I are so far behind the others that it should be called 'ridiculous' golf. One of those holes is just impossible, I declare loudly, and the little boy behind me sighs and whacks his ball straight into the hole. Meanwhile Mother's chortling behind the camcorder for posterity.

At least she films me finishing the Maze at the Theme Park, which is my one glory of the week.

Mother and Father are unbelievably perky all week, twenty-four hours a day, and they even give me money to buy everyone drinks at the end. It's a novelty to be so spoilt; my friend and I scrounge twenty fairground rides out of them and then run away – well, they are holding hands. Even money wouldn't coax me to be that embarrassed.

Much as I'd like to deny it, I suppose the holiday *might* be boring without them. No early mornings, no teasing, nobody to beat at golf (I did beat someone . . . in the end). No one to shoot in Battleships. Holidays are a blissful, chaotic state of affairs in the family. Next time I'm off to Ibiza . . . without them.

> 'Every year Jesus' parents travelled to Jerusalem for the Feast of Passover. When he was twelve years old, they went up as they always did for the feast. When it was over and they left for home, the child Jesus stayed behind in Jerusalem, but his parents didn't know it. Thinking he was somewhere in the company of pilgrims, they journeyed for a whole day and then began looking for him among relatives and neighbours. When they didn't find him, they went back to Jerusalem looking for him. The next day they found him in the temple . . . his parents were upset and hurt. His mother said, "Young man, why have you done this to us? Your father and I have been half out of our minds looking for you".'
>
> Seems like holidays were never straightforward and simple affairs, even for Jesus and his parents. Thank you, God, though, that you give us cause to celebrate and relax. Help us to make the most of times together and help us to put up with each other!

1997: Our Very Wonderful baby

The mother's view

The other Saturday, Anna was up before nine and showered and hard at work by ten. As she normally refuses to admit the existence of Saturday mornings, this was something of an event. And the reason for all this activity – a new addition to the Hinds family and one which is causing much excitement at least on the distaff side. The new arrival is very beautiful, of German extraction and we've christened her Daisy. She's white, twenty-three years old ... and have you guessed it yet? That's right, she's a Beetle of the Volkswagen variety.

For months, with her seventeenth birthday getting ever closer, Anna had been haranguing us about getting a Beetle. Mike had no intention of exchanging our old but trusty Montego for an even older and probably less trusty rustbucket until, with fortuitous timing, he became the proud owner of a brand new company car. Knowing that he, at least, would have a comfortable car to drive, he became much more amenable to the arguments put forward by both Anna and me. Beetles are viewed as the height of cool by all Anna's soulmates and as the children view me as slightly scatty anyway, an eccentric little car suits me rather well, bringing back memories of my first car, a Morris Traveller.

After much furtive scheming, we finally found what we hope is the right one. Ignoring the pessimists on all sides who shake their heads and tell us how uncomfortable they are and how expensive spares are, we are in the throes of first love. That Saturday morning, the day after we got her, Anna spent at least four hours washing, polishing, hoovering and just sitting in Daisy.

The main fault we've found so far is that the radio doesn't work but that's not a serious problem: the noise from the engine more than compensates for it. By the time you read this though, Anna will have started driving lessons, maybe even taken her test, and then, when she's on the road, my real problems will start. I can foresee arguments over priority of use but at the moment Anna and I are of one accord: besotted with our Beetle.

The daughter's view

Daisy is my new baby. I have turned into a cosseting mother overnight. I have video footage of every inch of her; photos, and pictures of her cover everything from my school files to the bathroom window. I must run outside for a chat with her twice a day, come rain or snow. I must polish her and keep her spotless. And of course I must tell everyone about her.

Daisy is a 1300 VW Beetle. Beetles went into production in 1945 and Daisy was born in 1973; so whatever my cynical friends and family think, she does have heating, a radio and even carpet. She is perfect.

She was also a complete surprise. I can't believe my parents managed to keep her a secret, although I was rather naïve, especially when we drove to her house and Dad was shown her workings. My mother maintained throughout that she was totally clueless about what was happening, and I was sucked in. My father always winds me up, so even when he opened our car door and told me he was taking our new car home, I didn't believe him. That beautiful Beetle? Yeah, right, Pa.

I felt compelled to stay in the street hugging Daisy when I found out. Hysteria is an understatement.

Daisy is supposed to be shared between my mother and me. Hopefully she'll not be too much in demand; I'm desperate to park her outside school. She will be terrible to drive I expect, and break down all the time, but it will be worth it. After all, she is the most beautiful car the world has ever seen. Men are going to be falling at her tyres everywhere.

I can't learn to drive for another month yet; we can't get Daisy insured until I'm of age; we can't even have her tuned up 'till then. It's torture! Meanwhile, I pace the house grasping my Highway Code, sit in Daisy pretending, spend my Saturdays washing and polishing her, and booking my tests (because I have my provisional licence ready to use on my birthday). I must pass first time – for Daisy.

Putting the 'L' in life

The mother's view

'You've stopped a bit close to the car in front, haven't you? You're supposed to be able to see tarmac.'

The driving lessons have only just started and Anna is already questioning my driving ability.

'I can see tarmac; you can't because you're in the back.'

Relieved that this time at least I am in the clear, I finish the drive home smugly.

Such was Anna's eagerness to learn to drive that, several weeks before her seventeenth birthday, her father and I both had the dubious pleasure of taking her to almost deserted car parks to get the feel of the car. Unwisely I chose a car park near the beach with the result that our lessons were punctuated with comments like these:

'You're getting a bit close to the cliff edge, Anna.'
'You are braking, aren't you?'
'Anna, STOP!'

But if that was scary, it was nothing compared to the real thing: hitting the road. Now I know what the 'L' stands for: L ... et me out of this car!

Driving a car is something I take so much for granted that it's easy to forget what's involved. Anna's comments that she can't change gear, steer and keep her eyes on the road all at the same time are a sharp and timely reminder of that. (The problem is compounded because she has to wave at other Beetle drivers — we've discovered a whole new family since acquiring Daisy).

But I have to say that I have a new-found respect for driving instructors. Even with the benefit of dual controls, it takes a very special person, with nerves of steel and tremendous patience, to spend hours each day in a car with learner drivers. I'm not that sort of person. I'm inclined to close my eyes which isn't altogether helpful, but fortunately her dad is made of sterner stuff and takes Anna out for the practice she needs in between her 'proper' lessons.

She has already passed her theory test and can't wait for the day when she's Queen of the Road. When that day comes, the best thing I can do is hand over the controls and say, 'Keep her safe, Lord.'

The daughter's view

According to my family, *my* opinions on my driving are completely and utterly misplaced. I know this because whenever I drive anywhere, the passengers in the back seats leave fingernail scratches and tortured slogans like 'We're all going to DIE!!!!' in the steam on the windows. My best friend – who I expected to at least try to hide her fear – refuses to come in my car anymore. I think my father is going to have to get a strong prescription of medication for stress if this goes on much longer.

When I started driving in car parks before my birthday, my mother could cope with me. There were no road markings to follow, no other cars and only a huge expanse of driving space. My mother didn't *enjoy* it, but she could cope.

When I was released onto the roads, even my father needed a whole week to summon the courage to take me out. My driving instructor doesn't have these problems (I drive better with him . . . as I keep assuring my parents), and my father, being set on bringing me up well, forces himself to take me. But my mother is a different story. She is terribly, terribly afraid. For her, letting me drive the five-minute journey home from school is a white-knuckled roller-coaster with the wild witch of the West. Admittedly, I cruelly broke speed limits and provided the appropriate soundtrack, like at the races, when I first discovered her weakness. But now I'm fairly kind. I've only just managed to drag her out on a main road, and I think she coped (albeit blindly) with the pure terror it affords. She coped admirably with my failure to brake in time, my lack of alertness and my assumption that everyone else will stop to let me through. She coped quite well with my jerky gear-changes, my narrow misses of the kerb and stalling at traffic lights. I think that the relief she feels when I pass my test will make up for the months of tension beforehand. She will never have to sit in a car beside me again. She will be able to worry from safely indoors, pacing the house.

My driving instructor tells me I can take my test in three weeks. I hope they're ready for me. Maybe I'll improve by then. If all else fails, I'll blame the car.

> 'During the last days of Jesus' life on earth, he offered up prayers and petitions with loud cries and tears to the one who could save him from death . . . and he learned obedience from what he suffered.'
> Hebrews 5: 7-8
>
> Dear God, I know what it's like to receive what seems like no answer from you. In response to my most desperate prayers and tears you sometimes appear to be silent. But from what I hear, Jesus felt ignored too – and of course you knew what you were doing, all along. Help me to trust you to do the best for me, and leave my prayers in your hands.

Shop 'till you drop

The mother's view

I came out of Sainsburys on Friday evening, which would have been all right except I went in on Wednesday morning. Okay, that's an exaggeration: it was actually Thursday morning.

They've changed the layout you see. They're extending and refurbishing the store and nothing is where it was, so the usual trek round on automatic pilot doesn't work. The meat is where the baked beans were, the bread is where the cheese was, and I never did find the talcum powder. I did meet a number of people I hadn't seen for years; they were probably lost in the last reshuffle. Dropped out of time and space, condemned to search perpetually for the Holy Grail or Barbie-shaped noodles in tomato sauce.

I don't like shopping; I don't like change. Put the two together and I rapidly turn into the 'poor old biddy wandering round talking to herself' to be avoided at all costs. It's bad enough when the packaging is changed and I have to stop, study the various packets of muesli, and think whether I normally buy deluxe with 35 per cent fruit, extra fruity with 40 per cent fruit or totally fruity with 99 per cent fruit. It's so much easier when you can just reach out and grab without thinking.

And it's not just food shopping I dislike. Me and clothes don't get on. Put me in baggy jumper and jeans and I'm happy but, unfortunately, that's not the sort of gear that goes down well at weddings. Last time I left it to the last minute to buy an outfit (even the word 'outfit' sits uneasily on my page) and, in desperation, I ended up buying two. I wore the second one and soon wished I'd worn the first. Neither of them are likely to be worn again.

Christmas shopping is another nightmare. I like the idea of finding 'just the right gift', but my enthusiasm is inversely proportional to time spent. Fifteen minutes trying to decide whether Auntie Doreen would prefer the cute purple spotted elephant or the discreetly elegant table mats, is enough to send me out swearing if I hear 'Winter Wonderland' once more this century...

However, there is one sort of shop I love and would happily spend hours and pounds in (if I had enough of either) – bookshops. Take me there and leave me there, now, please; I need to recuperate.

The daughter's view

'Do we have to go home now? ... Well, can we go the long way so I can go past the gorgeous bloke with the jeans sign again? Please?' Mother sighs and follows me up the road.

'He's a bit short for you,' she comments as we walk slowly past him. Mothers, eh.

But she's tireless, my mother is. I used to subject her to hours of gruelling changing-rooms, sweat and tears, and all she ever got was to use her credit card. Only when we got home would she realise the full extent of the damage, inspecting the price labels lying on the floor while I paraded carelessly.

One day I had a marvellous idea. Shopping trips were getting a bit thin on the ground, and I needed some new clothes. An allowance! The parents agreed and, after negotiation, the money duly went into my bank account. Sublime shopping sprees followed – my friends getting more annoyed than my mother used to – and followed, and followed, and followed. Then the bomb hit. I needed things, I mean proper things, sensible things like a new coat and school stuff. I went out, typed in my bank number, and the machine refused to give me money. It didn't respond to pleading or coaxing like my mother does ... and I couldn't face asking the bank lady again. Muttering about overdrafts, I had to go home, empty-handed.

Well, this hit hard, and fast. Shopping has become a rare treat. Real shopping, anyway. I have to make my fun from buying paper and new tights. Yesterday I bought eight pounds' worth of make-up, genuine, four-pounds-for-two-ounces stuff, and that'll have to last me for ages. When I go shopping, I do it properly.

My mother, on the other hand, is the complete opposite. For her, shopping for clothes is just a nightmare. With one week until my cousin's wedding, I had to take her out and force her to put an end to the endless, futile shopping trips. She just can't do it. She can't make a decision. With me, if I have the money, I'll take anything and everything that *might* be suitable. My mother probably has about three good outfits that she's bought in the past five years, and those were for weddings. But oddly, although I've offered, she's not keen to let me help her buy more.

> 'Why spend money on what is not bread, and your labour on what does not satisfy?' Isaiah 55:13

The best days of your life?

The mother's view

School, aah, memories. The 'cowsheds', wood and glass classrooms, wonderful in summer but not so hot in winter, would undoubtedly be condemned by environmental health officers today. One of the last all-girl grammar schools in town. Netball pitches, gymnasium but little else. Hockey meant a route march to the top of the hill to a public recreation ground, where our bodies were exposed to the elements and our navy knickers exposed to any strangers who had the misfortune to pass by.

School dinners in the canteen, chips once a month, if you were lucky, or not – for these were chips like no other chips you had ever tasted, or wanted to taste. Carefully planned menus cooked to deprive them, and us, of any nutritional good. Until at last in the sixth form, if you were very brave and could face the wrath of the headmistress, a large-busted, formidable lady, you could take sandwiches.

The teachers, invariably 'Miss' and powdery except for the geography mistress. Not only was she married, fat and fun, she had two sons of the right age. Which brings us to the token male teachers. The wild-haired Welshman who couldn't understand why pubescent girls showed so little interest in the glories of Latin; the smooth but greasy biology teacher whose slanty eyes followed you around class.

Though why we imagined any man would ever be interested in us with our navy pleated gymslips previously modelled by sacks of potatoes. Then the full force of the sixties hit even the backwoods of Wales and skirt lengths dropped and rose, and rose, more frequently than it rained. Teachers' pet monitors were appointed to measure skirt lengths and letters were sent home.

Some things it seems haven't changed. Anna spent her lower sixth year arguing with teachers over the length of her skirt. First it was too long, then too short, then she started avoiding the teachers.

I'm a supporter of school uniform, mainly because it gets rid of the 'what am I going to wear?' dilemma, and if I thought her skirt was offensively short, I'd do something. As it is I can't see what the problem is. She's polite, hard-working, and a credit to the school.

I'm proud of the way she looks, proud of her academic achievements, and most of all proud of her for who she is.

The daughter's view

I scuttle down the corridor, behind someone's flapping coat, ears pricked, body poised to run for it. The head-of-year's office door is open. Sweat saturates the air. I carry on, wincing, past the room.

'Anna!'

I turn around slowly. It's too late. I yank the rings off my fingers and hitch my skirt up. I trot humbly into his office.

He lets rip. My shirt's untucked, my hair's too bright, there're too many earrings in one ear, my skirt's too long, my cardigan's the wrong colour, my boots are too high, too many rings, and please don't feel that I'm trying to get at you.

He can't believe that I don't break the rules on purpose. I tried my best to find a nice cardigan and skirt, I toned my hair down for this term, my ears will heal up without rings, my old shoes are too small, and I can't afford to dye my hair again let alone replace my entire uniform.

Despite letters from Mummy and arguing with me ferociously, he will not learn. He will keep pestering me. All I want really is to pass my exams. But he's concerned with far more important things. When he's away I think he leaves a memo on his desk to the other teachers: don't let Anna Hinds get through a day without being nagged.

So I must behave like a hunted animal, avoid them, show my face only in lessons, and be the quietest person in the whole sixth-form Common Room. This is hard, especially when everyone else I see is breaking the rules too; so if you hear an indignant muffled shriek, don't worry. It's just me giving away my hiding place.

If you hear an older-sounding shriek, then that'll be my mother, in the middle of a letter complaining about me hiding. She's on my side in the battle of the rules, although I don't let her make an appearance to support me – it'll reveal her true feeble nature – it's better for her to feign fierceness from the cover of home. She knows they're all baddies and she knows that I really do want to finish my courses despite this. The Big Bad Head of Year has won himself some opposition – so he'd better look out.

> 'O! When she's angry she is keen and shrewd.
> She was a vixen when she went to school:
> And though she be but little, she is fierce.'
> From *A Midsummer Night's Dream* – Shakespeare
>
> Dear Daddy, calm me down, make me humble, shut me up; tame the vixen inside of me; and give me laughter when it gets tough.

1998: Fever pitch

The mother's view

One evening on a little French campsite in the summer of 1998, a middle-aged Welsh woman discovered Fever Pitch. It came as quite a surprise. I never expected to see myself in a bar, surrounded by chanting, face-painted Englishmen, let alone joining in, 'Meat pie, sausage roll, come on England, give us a goal!' Come to that, I never expected to see Anna with an English flag painted on her cheek, yelling with the best of them, and arranging her schedule to fit in with match times.

The reason for all this unprecedented behaviour was the England versus Argentina World Cup elimination game, which happened during our holiday (who in their right minds takes a holiday in France during a football tournament held in France?). England had struggled through so far, and seemed certain to be beaten by their old rivals (remember Maradona's 'hand of God'?) but, in the event, they were transformed and played like men possessed, even after Beckham was sent off in the second half.

And, of course, events on the pitch were treated with the appropriate response in the bar. As a man, we rose to celebrate the good times, sang our hearts out to 'Three Lions' in the interval, and were part of something greater than the individual. There was no way England could lose with so much 'hwyl'* in the room. But lose they did, on penalties, again, and it just wasn't fair!

I found it hard to sleep that night, and not just because of the late-night mourners returning to their tents. I kept going over the events in my mind, replaying it, if only this, if only that. They deserved to win and they hadn't. 'We don't always get what we deserve,' my old granny used to say, and most of the time, we should be grateful for that.

But I don't think I'll ever forget that night. I'm writing this a month after the event and I can't actually remember the score, but I do remember that sense of belonging, togetherness, the spirit of the blitz. And most of these were stereotypical English football fans, the sort who think if you say something loud enough the barman will understand but he won't understand your jibes about his personal hygiene because he's only a froggie. Whatever our differences in normal life, for a short while, we had a common bond. It aroused our passion, stirred our emotions. We cared about something outside ourselves. We cheered together, laughed together; and almost cried together.

If only we could bring fever pitch to church.

---

*Hwyl: a Welsh term – if I have to explain it, you won't understand.

The daughter's view

I was proposed to during the Brazil-Holland game this year. This sounds quite good (that's why I opened with it) but actually wasn't. I was busy (a) shushing him so I could see properly — excitement was rising as it was extra time — and (b) trying to look over my shoulder to pretend he was talking to someone else, since my parents were right in front of me. Mother was busy slapping Dad's head: 'Michael, your daughter's being proposed to'.

I don't like distractions during tense match moments — well, does anyone? My friends called over unexpectedly during England-Romania, and I shut them in the study and returned to the football, hopping back during the interval.

I don't pretend to be a big footy fan, or to watch anything except the Euro and World matches. I do not know what 'offside' means (yes, I've seen the sketches. I just refuse to believe that *anyone* understands). I do not shout technical things. Comments I make are simple, of the 'they don't have the ball enough', or 'their defence is rubbish' or 'there's nobody to pass to' variety. Y'know: they're the shouts of a girly supporter who wears the national flag on her face and gets really excited and might even sing *Three Lions*, but doesn't actually care about proving her footy knowledge. Who doesn't watch to talk about it afterwards and impress lads (I wouldn't — I'd sound silly), but who just can't help wanting to watch the matches. I don't approve of wives tagging along to a match with their husbands because it's the only time they get to see them. My mum came to a match in the pub with me this year because Dad had a headache.

We were in France for some of the time — Robert attempted to start a riot in the streets when France beat Italy, but the Frenchmen were having none of it — they drove around deep into the night tooting their horns. Pesky French.

I don't love Michael Owen, either. He's very sweet and everything, I just don't need or want another distraction. I love him for England; he's part of the team I paint the flag on for, but I love all equally and without unfair bias.

The one thing which annoys me is the ridiculous amount of money manifesting itself on a football field: millions of pounds for the players alone, plus huge sponsorship deals, and meanwhile the News jumps from World Cup to Famine In Africa in seconds. That kind of money could practically pull a whole country out of distress, but instead it's pulling footy hooligans. It's a grossly over-idolised hobby. At least some of us can appreciate that it's just a bit of excitement with a piece of leather! Well, sometimes we can.

> I've seen it on video, Lord, some of those church meetings always somewhere else, where passion for you takes precedence over all else. I've even been in meetings which come close to it where people are transformed by your Spirit. Help me Lord, not to be luke-warm but to care passionately about you, your people and your world. Bring your Church to fever pitch.

En vacances (Postcard from France)

The mother's view

Thirty-six hours, that's all it took. Less than two days on French soil before Anna discovered the delights of the off-licence section in the local supermarché: peach liqueur at £2.50 and a Malibu lookalike for £4. Her screams of delight caused near, and far, shoppers to look on in bemusement. Her pleasure was short-lived when her cruel parents said, 'no, you can't try them all, at least not at once.' However, we pointed out that, legally-speaking, she could take home as much as she wanted. Again her joy was cruelly snatched away when we said that she'd have to pay for it.

As it turned out, the wannabe Malibu was a disappointment, as was, inevitably, the £1.25 Cabernet Sauvignon. Although, after three-quarters of a bottle, Mike decided it didn't really taste too bad.

I'm not sure whether I would be capable of going through so much suffering for so little pleasure but there are times when being teetotal is a definite disadvantage. For instance, if my judgement was ever so slightly impaired, my navigation skills might be better. I blame the French system of putting signposts just after the road you want, and blatantly denying the existence of the village you know should be next. And it would help if roads were painted the same colour as they are on maps. At least then I might have some idea. As it is, I close my eyes just for a second, and next thing, Mike is yelling, 'which turning is it?' or 'do I go straight on here?' I choose a road at random, realise it is the wrong one – the late signpost again – and the screeching of brakes is accompanied by deep sighs. Half the time I'm sure he knows his way full well and is just using the occasion to prove his male superiority in all matters motoring.

And assuming we eventually arrive at a destination, chosen or unexpected, we then undergo the pleasure of a family outing. If you think 'undergo' suggests a visit to the dentist for a particularly nasty filling, and isn't appropriate to a family outing, then you obviously don't have children. Just because it's no longer necessary to carry a spare everything, toys to amuse, snacks to tempt, and general emergency supplies, doesn't mean your problems are over. You've then reached the 'what have we got to come here for? how long are we staying? is it time to go home yet?' stage. Your enthusiasm for a flower garden or ancient monument doesn't seem to have affected your children, and dragging them around after you is, on the whole, more trouble than it's worth. Better to save your pleasures for your old age, and resign yourself to days at the pool, or playing pool.

'Yes, thanks, we had a great holiday.'

The daughter's view

... Speaking of masochism, the showers here must define it. They are open air, with push-tap mechanisms, and they bring a whole new meaning to the term 'massaging shower-head'. It's pot-luck every morning to get hot water, and faced with all this and the daunting scramble-across-the-campsite-in-nightie, I think I'd almost prefer to use the cold tap behind the tent. At least it's hidden.

Furthermore (I'll only whinge for a little bit longer) people speaking a language I don't understand are unbearable to live with. I can't eavesdrop, which makes me uneasy all the time and very paranoid. ('They're laughing at me! They're laughing at my bikini! Yes, they definitely are!') The best thing they do is make bread, and only then if you catch it at the right moment. The wine, although dirt-cheap, is rubbish. (At least they do have some choice: there's Bacardi and Baileys in plentiful supply.) The management on the campsite refuse to co-operate with us British tourists (expect they feel similarly about us), and instead of telling us they don't understand what we mean when we ask for something, they just refuse to give it us. Usually when it's right there under their noses.

Living with family is also another letter full of grumbling. Close proximity = not happy families! Dad seems to be the worst sleeper these days, it used to be the boys and Harvey, a few years ago. Now Harvey's in the kennels this year, and Rob and Neil seem to have quietened. But Dad gets up in the night, snores, and rises at the crack of dawn. Also, I get to enjoy the loud noise of foreign radio in the inconsiderate hours from next-door, me being stuffed in the bedroom right at the back corner of the tent. Ooh, I hate being that close to other people.

Still, the country itself can't help being populated with silly holidaymakers, and it *is* beautiful. Lazy and relaxed, and time seems to slow down (despite the manic drivers on the roads round here – do they *have* a speed limit?). It's so quiet, there are often no people at all on the streets when we drive around. The houses are quaint too, little white stone efforts with thatched or red-clay tiled roofs, and cute little rows of lavender or vineyards surrounding them. You should see the beach. It's so long and curvy and golden (much like my tanned legs ... ahem!), and the evening is the best time to go, when the crowds are thinning and the sky is perfectly clear. The promenade is uncluttered, all there is to spoil the view are huge white apartment blocks, but they're set a little way back, so you can turn your back on them and it's unspoilt. I tried to persuade Dad to buy one, an apartment I mean, they range between about £11-20,000. I checked in the estate agent. Lots of young people have had the same idea as me, 'cause at night they're out on the balconies with wine, playing Garbage at a low volume. If the French and the Tourists didn't live here, I'd be out here like a shot. Have to make my fortune, and start a war, first ... See you soon! Love Anna.

Dear God, Thanks for a great holiday. Amen.

R-Letter Day

The mother's view

In ten days time the A-level results will be out. We'll find out if it's to be the bright light delights of London, the salty sea breezes of Southampton, or a return to school for resits. The strain is beginning to tell. Anna has her heart set on University College London, much to Dad's disgust who sees a multiplicity of £ signs in his frequent nightmares. 'What's wrong with Southampton? It was good enough for me.'

There's nothing really wrong with Southampton. Like UCL, it's a good university, and both have excellent English departments. It's just not London. So Anna's talking about resitting if she doesn't get the grades she needs. Which brings us to the crunch: the grades. She needs an A and two Bs, which isn't quite as bad as the two As and a B needed by her friend, but is bad enough. I said, 'in ten days, all will be decided,' but that's only true if she gets those grades; if not, then the stress of reality will bite. We're still at the 'what if' stage, where there's hope, but if that goes, what then?

Secretly I'm optimistic, but I don't want to put the pressure on, to make her feel she's let us down if she doesn't achieve what I know she's capable of. I suspect, though, that I've gone to the other extreme of making her feel that I don't expect her to do well. It's a difficult balance. Ah, well, we'll know soon enough.

R-Day minus 1

When Anna sat her exams back in June, it seemed like a lifetime before the results would be out, now the day is nearly upon us. I've spent the morning cleaning parts of the kitchen which haven't seen a j-cloth for years. It was the only antidote I could think of for the churning stomach blues. My friend was on holiday in Greece when her daughter's results came out. Why can't I be that detached? We've been through every possible combination of grades, and the necessary actions they would entail, except the one she's, we're, hoping for. That would be tempting fate.

The kitchen's sparkling; my stomach's still churning. Why pay for colonic irrigation when you can get it for free?

The daughter's view

Dear A-Level Examiner,

    I write to explain my reasons for asking you to screw up my exam paper and throw it away, or even better, burn it without trace. Forgive what may seem an unusual request from a mentally unstable candidate. You may have received my postcard from France, and following that, the small sum of money wrapped up in brown paper, so you will know that I have not been in a healthy state since the end of June. I have reason to believe myself to suffer more than my fair due of panic. Yes, most A-level students suffer to some extent, but I am certain you will sympathise when I describe what must be worse than most people in the country... (Under normal circumstances my fingers are deft and do not produce that many full-stops where there should only be one; but they tremble violently). I have reason to suspect a heart murmur in what has always been a perfectly well functioning organ in my body. Further, nightmares and frantic panicking lead me to conclude that I am not your typical A-level prospect, and certainly not one with the mental or physical health to continue her education safely. I fear that the consequences, should I ever be forced to sit an exam again, or indeed to see my actual results, would be dire. Suicide looms in the future for such people who cannot handle the smallest of crises. I therefore beg you to reconsider your decision to send on my results to the school tomorrow; I believe that a life without them would be far less hazardous, and I am sure that you do not want to be held personally responsible for the loss of a (otherwise quite normal and happy) human life.
Yours faithfully,
A. Hinds.

PS Please forgive the shaky handwriting.

> I know in a few years' time, we'll look back on this and say, what was all the fuss about? But right now it matters. It shouldn't matter so much, but it does. 'And we know that in all things God works for the good of those who love him'. Help me step back.
>
> 'Who of you by worrying can add a single hour to his life?'
> Matthew 6: 27

Good job hunting

The mother's view

Once upon a time there was a fair maiden who dreamed of the golden streets of London. She worked hard and at last the day arrived when her dream came true. Too late, she discovered that, instead of gold, the streets of London were paved with many thousands of unsmiling, unhappy people, and so she returned to her cottage by the sea and looked for a new dream to dream.

And then her problems really started.

There's only so much sympathy and understanding you can offer, particularly when you're traumatised yourself, and the prospect of Anna hanging around the house for a year looms large. So we offered advice. Get a job; do work experience; investigate other universities; sign on; enrol on a course; do voluntary work; do anything except waste the year. Next thing we're accused of pressuring her into doing things she doesn't want to, which seems to be anything except bar work. So I bite my tongue and let her get on with it. And the days pass, and the weeks, and promises hang in the air, and mother is expected to drive her here, there and everywhere in her search for work.

Meanwhile I think perhaps it's time I found a job, did something useful for a change. Trouble is, I'm totally unqualified for life in the real world. Most jobs either I can't do or I wouldn't want to do. The few I'm sure I could do, I'm not given a chance, just because I don't have the qualifications or the experience – what do employers want, blood?

So it's back to the drawingboard, or keyboard in my case.

I suppose it makes sense to use what skills you have, and any talent I have, however little that may be, is in writing. I came to this remarkable conclusion just after a friend assured me that God had something for me just around the corner. Two days later, I was asked to consider ghost-writing an autobiography. The man who asked me, an ex-cop from New York, said, 'There's no such thing as coincidences.' (Don't you just love it when these ridiculously unlikely coincidences happen? A little Welsh woman and a Bronx patrolman sitting in a sandwich bar in Swansea.)

We know that God has plans for us, plans to give us hope and a future. As my future drops into my lap, I should be able to rest assured that God has Anna's life well in hand too.

The daughter's view

It's an inevitable equation. Unemployment leads to jobhunting, which leads to the depths of misery which leads to a quick-fix solution. Having the means to reach this solution becomes a necessity – which leads back to jobhunting, in desperation. To put it simply, in order to fund my frantic compulsive shopping drive, I must find a job. But it's a vicious circle. Ten per cent off! taunt the shop posters on the street leading to the Jobcentre. New U2 album out this week! Half price sale! Massive price slashes on jackets! No, no, no, sings my lickle pink purse, but yes, yes, yes, shout my hands as they fondle the goods. I make it as far as the Jobcentre, usually, even though it's quarter of an hour's walk from the bus station (and that's provided I walk fast and no window-shopping), in a positive state of mind: I've got a cheque in my bag to pay in to the bank, and I am going to be calm and controlled and think of the shopping I can do at Christmas. Addicts to spending, I feel, aren't just making it up and I realise I've got another addiction to add to my list. But anyway, the Jobcentre is nice and warm and I take a ticket to be seen, then wander amongst the other saggy-mouthed unemployeds to browse the racks (this bit's almost like shopping). After I pick out the most fun-sounding job descriptions and make my little list, sitting listening to the Unemployeds talking about joyriding cars (a B-reg Nova, last time I heard) and their Impending Marriages is as close as the Jobcentre gets to providing mild entertainment. Next, we are herded towards desks with our numbers in little flashing lights above them, and 'sorted out'. This is much like being packed into a number of different boxes at once, stuck together with sellotape and left with a label of instructions. These instructions lead us little boxes to different destinations: Monday the Travel Agent, Wednesday the Pub. The Jobcentre desk-person then sends us on our way. This is when I reach the danger zone. Far from being happy and safe in my little boxes (Little Boxes, on the hillside, Little Boxes, made of ticky-tacky), the urge to break free begins. It's the sense of hopeless shipping in circles that creates the misery. And as we all know, misery leads to shopping. This shopping, which I know must inevitably happen, I try to delay for as long as possible. At last, feeling encouraged by my own discipline and strength, and by the fact that after searching for an hour I have found the U2 album cheaper than anywhere else, I am able to justify the purchase. Sighing contentedly on the bus as I read the CD sleeve, I, still unemployed, return home as unfulfilled as when I left. It just doesn't feel like it.

> 'The Lord is close to the broken-hearted, and saves those who are crushed in spirit.' Psalm 34:18
>
> Save the people who walk through the doors of the Jobcentre, Daddy; and comfort and cheer them up in that way you do.

Man about the house

The mother's view

My husband thinks a lot of me. He tells me so. He tells me how he thought about getting me some flowers. He would have done but they'd have wilted if he'd kept them in his office all afternoon, or they'd have been squashed on the back of his bike, or it's too close to Mother's Day and the flowers in the shops are a rip-off. And anyway he grows me flowers, or at least he grows me courgettes. By the barrel-load. Still it shows he thinks of me, and, I suppose, after twenty years of marriage, I should be grateful for that.

He says it was his sporty blue MG that attracted me in the first place. In truth it was his dashing good looks. Stop laughing, Anna. Twenty years ago he had hair, and a muscular physique . . . and a sporty blue MG. When we got married he sold his MG to buy a cooker and carpets. Now that's love.

Twenty years on, it's a completely different sort of car that has him in its spell. Maintaining two Beetles requires a lot of dedication, and he's happy to oblige. We're thinking of buying him an anorak for Christmas. But while car maintenance takes his time in the winter, it's the garden in the summer. He's enthusiastic and he works hard in spite of the forces of destruction which manifest themselves in the form of children, footballs, slugs and a dog. The garden looks a picture in summer although this year's lawn edging of pink and orange Busy Lizzies doesn't quite work for me. Which brings me to honesty (stick with me, it'll all make sense soon, maybe.) We have a policy of expressing honest opinions, so if dinner isn't brilliant, Mike will say so, justifying himself by saying, 'It's much better like this because if I say something is excellent, you'll know I mean it, and I'm not just saying it.' Similarly he doesn't hold back when the children turn up with green or spiked hair. I try to conceal my dismay and avoid a quarrel. Mike's inherited his lack of tact from his father.

Their, nowadays good-natured, arguments started when Mike was in his teens, partly because Pop believes whatever he reads in the newspapers and can, and does, expound at great length on any topic. A wise man would sit back and say, 'Yes, Pop', but Mike can't resist the challenge. He responds in like fashion, throwing facts into the arena to disprove Pop's statements. The big difference is that Mike doesn't rely on unreliable newspapers; if he doesn't know something, he makes it up. He's very convincing too. Not that Pop listens, of course. Which is the same complaint that our children have started making about their father. Either that, or he doesn't understand. Mike's, and my, assertion that we do understand and we were young once, is humphed at in disbelief. If the children were asked for one of their father's catchphrases, I suspect they would offer, 'I'm only saying this for your own good.' Do they listen? Do they appreciate it? Well, they're turning out pretty well, so he must be doing something right.

He loves us, wants the best for us, can be unexpectedly understanding and sympathetic when it's needed, and grows amazing courgettes. What more could we ask for?

The daughter's view

My dad calls girls 'bits of crumpet'.

'She used to hit me when I said that,' (that's what he'll say when he reads this). It may've been a PC term back when my dad was wearing flares, I suppose.

He did wear flares. After a brief spell as a teddy boy, complete with drainpipe trousers and Brylcreem, it was flares and sideburns all the way. I have photos to prove it.

'I was *cool*,' he assures the children, who're trying to listen between laughing.

He still firmly believes this. Moving into the 90s, he's switched to 'I'm Too Sexy For My T-shirt' and fishermen's hats. He was reluctant to wear a t-shirt I bought him for Father's Day though, so perhaps his taste for bad taste has worn off just a little bit. It wasn't a very convincing cartoon of him, he doesn't wear a string vest after all. He did wear it in France, because less people would understand the words 'Sexy Man'. My mother on the other hand, wears her 'Away With The Fairies' with pride.

My dad teases my brothers about girls. Only 'cause they go red. He inquires about this or that 'bit of hot totty', or whether they 'got any action' or 'snogged'. I tell him most of the kinds of things my brothers won't. He doesn't get much of a go at embarrassing me. OK, so when he marches up the front of the pub in a football match to get a good view, and plonks his rump right in front of practically the whole audience, blocking all sunlight and sound, that's embarrassing. Slightly.

We're looking forward to the day when Dad turns into Grandad completely. He's showing promising signs at the moment, selective deafness and making-up-things-he-calls-facts being the best. As yet he hasn't come home drunk and fallen into the bath, but Dad's not a big drinker. He'll drink whisky and wine, which he shares with me now, and he's taken a partiality to my rum and Baileys. In fact I've changed my mind, he drinks too much. When it comes to my drinks cabinet, at least.

My dad doesn't shout at me about the phone bill anymore. (Well it did get rather tedious for one and all.) (Actually I really put that bit so he won't shout at me any more. Then it'll be true.)

My dad wants to visit old fishing towns on holiday, and places he knows about just so he can ramble on for hours.

My dad bought a video camera on a whim two years ago, purely for the sake of obtaining embarrassing footage at opportune moments. He's got some good stuff since then, because he's so good at sneaking around.

My dad's newest toy is our second Beetle, Brian. He reads books about Beetles, magazines about Beetles and maintenance manuals about Beetles. Even I don't go that far. He had a scaled-down DIY model for his birthday. My dad talks about the dryness of wine like he knows what it means (and I mean, anyone who thinks they understand that is just pretending).

My dad's a good pretender. For the sake of pretence, he'll totally fabricate an answer to any question ('Dad, how do you calculate the friction using Newton's Law?' [. . . after complicated, frantic sketching . . .] '. . . and later on you'll learn about logs, which are great fun . . .').

My dad's threatening to spend all our inheritance on cruises before he dies. (I'm putting him in the shed to live anyway.) He's hoping to live off the earnings of three very successful children.

He's a perfectionist.

'Dad, I had 98 per cent for my maths exam!'

'What happened to the other two per cent?'

Still, as Robert says, Dad failed his English O-level six times, so there's always that to fall back on.

My dad says that I have all of his worst faults, so this is both a father and daughter character sketch. I can put up with it, as long as I don't turn into Grandad . . .

> **Children, do what your parents tell you. This is only right. 'Honour your father and your mother' is the first commandment that has a promise attached to it, namely, 'so you will live well and have a long life'.** Ephesians 6:1-2 [taken from the Message]
>
> **Husbands, go all out in your love for your wives, exactly as Christ did for the church – a love marked by giving, not getting.**
> Ephesians 5:25 [taken from the Message]

Lurve

The mother's view

They don't write pop songs like they used to. (I'm sounding more like my granny every minute.) These days I'm lucky if I can pick out one word in ten; it's not like the old days when songs told a story. Remember 'Leader of the Pack' or 'Tell Laura I love her' or that grand old favourite 'No charge'? For those of you too young to recall that particular gem, it's about a little boy who presents his mum with a bill, 'for taking out the trash $2', that sort of thing. His mum looks at it, doesn't say anything but turns it over and starts to write her own invoice which goes something like this:

For carrying you for nine months	*No charge*
For changing stinky nappies by the score	*No charge*
For clearing up your sick	*No charge*

And so on. Only, of course, this was American syrup so it wasn't so crudely expressed!

I suppose all parents could come up with lists of things we've done at 'no charge'. As the children get older the tasks change. Who hasn't sympathised with the driver whose car carries the sticker 'Mum's taxi'?

And, of course, it's not just parents who do things for others. As children, friends, neighbours, colleagues, each one of us will do things for others without, necessarily, expecting reward. I added 'necessarily' there because certain tasks like weeding the paths go down better with a little sweetener. But to get back to the song, on the whole, it's true, parenting involves a lot of work for which we make no charge, and quite often get no thanks. Where I argue with the composer is when it comes to the last line, 'I guess the true cost of real love is no charge'.

Love which doesn't cost is worth nothing; it isn't love at all. The true cost of real love is high. Most relationships involve the investment of time, energy or money, but more than that, in a relationship of love the real cost is you. The physical work is nothing compared to the emotional toil involved. Giving yourself isn't cheap.

Why do we bother? Because we're made in God's image? Christ went further, gave more, in the name of love than most of us will have to.

The daughter's view

I love reading about Dougal because he's such a grumpy guts and he whinges noisily about everything in the world.

I love my baby Daisy because she puts all the other cars to shame and she toots her horn whenever she feels like it (or when there're old people on the road).

I love jelly babies because they taste nice.

I love my toes because they're long and bony and not-cute and they don't like nail varnish.

I love shopping for clothes because (I'm a girl) the feel of new clothes doesn't last long enough.

I love my brother Rob because he's cool and funny and he lets me twist his hair into spikes.

I love my old Converse trainers because they're completely out of fashion and they have big holes and they smell.

I love lightning because it's God's big magic show.

I love my Dad because he came down to see me when I turned up at his work and because he thinks he's trendy.

I love the way my hair looks when it's wet. I love all of my friends because they phone me every day when I'm ill.

I love words: fridge and tortoise and pants.

I love writing cheques because it's new.

I love playing pool even though I'm totally useless.

I love my brother Neilypoos because he plays the baby and because he trusts me.

I love reading books of quotes because I like to think I could quote them and sound intellectual.

I love card shops because I can stay in them for hours.

I love my 'bit of stuff' because (sorry to get soppy) he's gorgeous and treats me like a pwincess.

I love listening to The Muppet Show because it's silly, and I can DJ it.

I love walking around barefoot everywhere (until a STUPID WASP STUNG ME).

I love making coffee with things that are bad for me like Baileys, squirty cream or chocolate sauce and flake.

I love eating Dairylea straight from the foil because it tastes yummmmmmy and lasts for ages.

I love my mummy 'cause she's just like me and 'cause she's silly and limps when I've hurt my foot and doesn't do any housework at all. And 'cause she writes stuff that make my books worth publishing!!

| **'Love so amazing, so divine, demands my soul, my life, my all.'** Thanks heaps, Lord!

'In heaven an angel is nobody in particular'*

The mother's view

In heaven I'll be able to eat all the chocolate I want and never get fat. In heaven, it will only rain at night, there'll be no hormones or piles of ironing or greasy dishes. In heaven I won't have to put up with all the things and people who irritate me now. Not that I imagine that whatshername from the Post Office will be there anyway, and definitely not him from the bus stop, and as for that old harridan, no chance. What would really make it heaven would be God consulting me about who to let in. 'Look, he's the one who stole the last shopping trolley in Sainsburys on Christmas Eve, 1981. You're not coming in, yah boo sucks.'

Perhaps we'll all have little compartments of our own, each matched to our requirements – for me, a roaring fire, which never goes out of course, a big comfy armchair, and book-lined walls with an endless supply of slightly better than trashy novels, oh, and chocolate. We'll have regular but not too frequent visits from our loved ones who will greet us joyfully instead of sullenly mumbling, 'I'm starving, what's for tea?' And guilt will not exist.

Admittedly it could be a fairly exclusive place, this heaven of mine. Which somehow doesn't quite tie in with God's idea of heaven. He seems determined to persevere with the 'more the merrier' way of thinking. I have a feeling I'm going to be surprised when I see who's there. But it won't upset me if whatshername from the Post Office is there or him from the bus stop or the old harridan, because heaven's not like that. If a selfish, confused woman like me can be welcomed by the creator of the universe there's hope for everyone.

Did you notice I said 'confused'? Now you've probably read enough of me to say, 'You confused? Nonsense. We've never met a less-confused person(!)' And I agree, I wasn't confused, not so's you'd notice, until I started thinking about heaven. You see, according to *Chambers Dictionary*, heaven is, first and foremost, 'the vault of sky overhanging the earth'. Seven definitions further on, it adds that it could be 'supreme happiness'. Graham Kendrick says heaven is in my heart, while John Lennon preferred to imagine there's no heaven. I could go on but I'll leave you with this thought: if each of us has our own idea of what heaven will be like, how is God going to make us all happy? I'm glad I'm not God. And I bet you are too.

The daughter's view

When you wish (upon a star), makes no difference who you are, anything your heart desires will come to you. I think widowed rich women expect heaven to be like a million-dollar health suite, swamped with swelteringly fit naked men. Indian restaurant owners expect their customers to believe heaven to be just like the Sunday 'eat-as-much-as-you-like' with the same decor and piped sitar muzac. People who buy microwave meals for-one expect companionship and feasting, much like a Tesco aisle on Singles night. Children expect slides, balloons, chocolate ice-cream and no rules, except Los Angeles children who expect guns that shoot caps, free Jeeps with valet parking, and immortality. Dougal from *The Magic Roundabout* expects an endless round of tea and biscuits, and a lobotomised Zebedee. George Orwell probably expected heaven to be anti-Utopia, with as many problems as on earth and more besides, caused by every-one expecting all of the above. Film directors expect everyone to smile always and never need their noses dusting, and special effects at their fingertips, and a chair right next to The Boss with their names on. The Spice Girls expect a holi-day, but nothing material, I can only suppose. Angels probably suppose heaven to be something different to what they're in.

My mother expects heaven to be . . . somewhere with nothing to worry about, I think. Somewhere that she can do her relaxation practice in peace. Without people who call Dad away on business, without people who phone up selling conservatories or Jehovah's Witnesses who feel compelled to prey on feeble people like her who're scared to slam the door. Without the hassles of daily life, without Sainsburys changing the layout of their aisles or the packaging of white bread. Without sulky teenagers who want labels on their clothes, relatives who have to be talked to or people she doesn't like but also has to be polite to. Without people who can't spell 'Hinds'. Without dirt to ruin or rip clothes that she has to wash. With Radio 2 played all day, a nice big bed, the Archers, hair that behaves, a dog that doesn't run away, chocolate and Mel Gibson films. But don't we all expect heaven to be something like that?

'And in that heaven of all their wish, There shall be no more land, say fish.' Rupert Brooke

*G.B. Shaw

The demon drink

The mother's view

Take 6lbs of carrots, add a gallon of water and boil. Stir in sugar, yeast, raisins, wheat, orange, and lemon, and then pour down drain carefully. You could keep it for a year to mature but you might as well save yourself some time and room space; no one's going to drink it. Unless you've got an Uncle Bun. Uncle Bun is a kindly soul who doesn't like to hurt people's feelings and, after a pleasant New Year's Eve, will drink even a murky brown liquid masquerading as my mum's carrot whisky. Auntie Eva didn't appreciate it. She was trying to get him home, but as fast as she was putting one arm in his sleeve, he was taking the other out. Round and round he twirled like a happy smiling woodentop.

I come from a long line of drinkers. I'd better rephrase that. My family all liked a drink, a party, an opportunity for a sing-song. We numbered some fine voices in our midst, including a Male Voice chorister. (I can't sing; I don't drink – the thought occurs to me, belatedly, that perhaps I was a changeling.) However, even if the genes skipped a generation, they've re-emerged in my children, or, so far, in Anna at least. The drinking genes that is, they've managed to avoid the singing genes. Not that there was much hope of anything else – their father also comes from a long line of drinkers, as opposed to singers.

His favourite is malt whisky, the smokier and peatier the better. He's also very fond of red wine, though how anyone can enjoy a wine described as tasting 'like Ferrari tyres' beats me. Anna's taste is girlier: sweet white wines, chocolate vodka and coconut liqueur, that type of thing. The one tipple they agree on, and fight over, is Bacardi and Coke. 'Try this, you'll like it,' they say, every now and again, about something or another. I sniff, hold my nose, sip and ... spit. No, I don't really but I'd like to.

It's probably a good job that I don't drink though, I'd be an alcoholic by now. Anna spent the first six months of her life crying, causing me frequently to say, 'I could do with a drink.' Now I come to think of it, there are plenty of things today which have the potential to drive me to drink, Anna, Robert and Neil to name but three. The only liquid solace I have comes from the teapot. It's cheap, comparatively harmless, but it doesn't make me giggle helplessly. Maybe I should try harder – all those people can't be wrong, surely?

The daughter's view

I was cleaning the dining-room (had to mention that somewhere) just now. The dining-room is where the alcohol is kept, in a big cupboard, you see. It's a pretty place, like a fairyland, with a glass shelf full of different kinds of glasses, a huge mirror covering the back, and of course, stacks of lovely bottles. Bacardi lids, which I am collecting, are strewn about. The bottles are happily full and large (the best way for any bottle to be). It was a hard job not to take some out, but I kept repeating to myself: *It's one o'clock in the afternoon. One o'clock*. If I did begin in the afternoon, then I'd know my days of sobriety were truly over. (My family would say they already are.) Not that there's anything wrong with beginning things in the afternoon. For example, the day is best begun after noon. Cleaning isn't really a morning job either. However, alcohol is an evening pastime, for some reason. The earliest I'd start (demands of sobriety command this) is five ('cause that's when Happy Hour commences in the Miami cocktail bar in town). Happy Hour is the most appropriate title ever in the whole wide world; nothing makes me happier than a half-price Baileys cocktail.

Mother is celibate. No, that's not right. Mother doesn't drink. Teetotal. That sounds like a golf word. If I can't remember the techno-jargon then how am I supposed to even consider following her example? Besides, wine is good for you. 'Tis. My lickle brother says solemnly: Alcohol is bad for you. No, I scold, (he must learn): It's not. It makes you smile. Neil nods and runs off to ask Uncle Kevin to buy him another pint.

Who wants to play with children who don't?

Anyway. Mother's celibacy (I get them confused not because they sound similar, but because they mean the same ... denial. I'm one but not the other, but I still don't like the sound of either.) is going to make it hard for her to write about drink as a topic. Tea? Orange juice? She's not ever been drunk, but she could write about Other Peoples' Mishaps. Getting stuck in the bath (mentioning no names), or Dad's drunken escapades of which there are many. Dad was left propped up against his front door many nights as a youngster, following a contented evening of switching front gates and traffic-coning the roads. All I have done is knock on a door or two, renditions of seventies' numbers in karaoke, oh, and I howl at the moon sometimes. That's nothing – you should hear some of my friends' stories. I'm not ashamed; oh no not I. I will survive, and happily, too.

> **A laughing, singing, having-fun Jesus isn't an image that readily springs to my mind. Gentle, compassionate, loving, yes, but party-going? But party-go he did and what's more, when the wine ran out, he fixed it. It gives a different perspective to the man.**

Ambrosia

The mother's view

I really should go on a diet. I say that to myself or anyone who wants to listen at least once a week. It's not that I think I'm grotesquely fat or even particularly overweight, it's just that I seem to be losing control of my eating habits. I'm at home during the day, supposedly writing a bestseller, and every time writers' block strikes (at least twice an hour) I head for the kitchen.

First things first, I fill the kettle. Once the tea's brewing, I decide I'd better have a biscuit to accompany it. Looking in the biscuit jar I discover, surprise, surprise, they're my favourites, malted milks, ideal for dunking. I eat one while I'm waiting and then take another two, or better still three, to dip in my tea and suck.

I'm beginning to suspect that I'm addicted to tea. I tried the decaffeinated variety a while ago. My friend suggested that I break myself in gently and alternate the decaff with the regular sort, but that sounded a wimpish thing to do. I favoured the clean break technique. After three weeks of decaff and three weeks of permanent headache, I gave up and returned to my daily overdose of tannin and caffeine. Still, at least, it's Fair Traded tea, so I'm doing my bit for the Third World, aren't I?

And then lunchtime. Everyone knows there's no such thing as a small piece of cheese, and if I'm having cheese, I'd better have crisps to go with it, and a pear would be nice, and a banana, and you really need something sweet to end on, now where are those biscuits, and so it goes on, and on, through the day.

I tell myself, as I tuck into my third banana of the day, that fruit doesn't count. It's good for me. All those vitamins and fibre and stuff, I should be brimming over with life and vitality. Perhaps I could blame my metabolism: all that fruit is being transformed into fat globules instead of nuggets of energy. Some part of the process is definitely going wrong. Yes, that's it.

Anna, meanwhile, would claim that as a vegetarian she has a better diet than the rest of us. She forgets to mention that she doesn't like cheese or eggs, and isn't that keen on vegetables, which goes to make balanced meal planning an exercise which would test the skill of a first class dietician. Generally she survives on chips, crisps, curry and chilli. Still she seems to thrive on it.

Now that's done, it must be time for a cup of tea.

The daughter's view

11.07 am: **Thinks:** *Sure it's not morning yet. Just 'cause it's daylight – oh, pants, better get up, I'll miss the Teletubbies.*
Eats: Rice Crispies (1 bowl) without sugar. **Thinks:** *Eh-oh, Po. Eh-oh, Laa-Laa. Ooh look, it's nearly lunchtime.*

11:57 am: **Thinks:** *Pants, have to go out to the garage in slippers to fetch veggie food. Pants pants pants – oh, Robert, sweetie ...* **Eats:** (fetched by Robert) 1 microwave-for-one Heinz Cuisine (tagliatele with peas and carrots and baked beans in a cheese sauce. Nicer than it sounds), plus orange juice, plus lickle tin of peaches. **Thinks:** *What a good healthy lunch. I do feel cleansed.*

2:34 pm: **Thinks:** *Do you ever get the feeling you need something? ... No, not exercise. I don't think I'm hungry, but I've got nothing to do ... Oh, well I'll eat anyway.* **Eats:** another can of peaches and a slug of Bacardi (to start the writing processes up). **Thinks:** *Yaay, she's workin', she's movin' ...*

6:17 pm: **Thinks:** *Maybe I'll do some work after tea. I always feel more alert in the night. I'll dance around to 'Chim Chiminee' first ...* **Eats:** Whatever the family have, minus dessert (diet effort), followed by a healthy-sized rum 'n' coke (to ease along the writing processes). **Thinks:** *When did anyone ever stop at one? ...*

When did anyone ever stop at one? Oh, although I've got a pack of ten jam doughnuts that go off tomorrow, I'll just eat *one* because I'm sensible. So we refrain for the sake of our waists *in* the house, but *outside* the house is just as bad. At a free feed, for example, you *should* eat until you're past full, shouldn't you? You *should* be able to eat until you're about to burst and splatter everyone else in the room with bits of your satisfied tummy. If the bar's complimentary, or you're in a hotel being paid for by someone else, then why *can't* we eat and eat and eat? If someone's paying, that's 'cause *they* can afford it and *we* can't – it makes sense to gorge, gorge, gorge. Not that I can talk – if you'd found me at my grandparents' anniversary party last month, you would have seen nothing but one scant plateful delicately devoured.

Some people, though (notably my dad – how embarrassing) are unabashed at mealtimes. They realise the need to feed and won't let little things like manners get in the way.

Old ladies have this sussed and small children have this sussed, but people with etiquette just go hungry. 'Tis indeed a sad state of affairs. But nevertheless, we *have* to be civilised and we *have* to eat only one mince pie, no matter how many times they're wafted under our noses. Ah, society. How cruel it is.

At home it's just the same if you're paying: those mince pies (a box of twenty) go off, but the last scrape of margarine goes further and the bread lasts those extra few days. I expect my diet to be greatly improved, or greatly strained when I leave home. Meanwhile, I'm frantically taking advantage of my parents, who wish to pay until I'm full!

In a country where obesity and eating disorders are becoming more common, it's easy to be flippant and take food for granted.

Thank you, Lord, for the food we eat and the bread of life.

The only way is up

The mother's view

When I was little I wanted to be a vet. That was until I saw a television programme in which a vet had his hand stuck up a cow's bottom. That succeeded in destroying both my image of vets as people who spent their time helping nice cuddly furry little things, and also any ambition I had in that direction.

Later I decided I'd be an engineer. I'm not sure what set me on that course, the only thing I can think of is a television programme, the name of which I forget now, about oil rigs. I really wanted to own an oil company, and becoming an engineer was the only way I could see myself getting anywhere near that ideal, as my mum said the bank probably wouldn't lend me enough money to buy one outright. I didn't see that being totally unmechanically-minded was a great problem for an engineer. Miss Loxton, my careers teacher, thought otherwise.

By now, of course, Jacques Cousteau was on our television screens. (It's rather worrying, the way my life seems to have been directed by whatever happened to be on the screen at any particular moment!) That settled it for me. A life in or on or under the ocean waves beckoned. I suffered from sea-sickness, couldn't swim awfully well, and didn't like putting my head under the water, so sailing and deep sea diving weren't really options. I settled for the next best thing – a degree in oceanography.

Now this was back in the early seventies, when openings for second-rate oceanographers were few and far between, and I ended up in the civil service working as a computer programmer. Which is where I met Mike, and took up full-time motherhood and housewifery, which was probably what I always wanted anyway.

So much for then, what about now? With my creative juices having been released, I suppose my ambition should be to be a best-selling author. Most days however, my main ambition is to survive to the end of that day. Otherwise my ambitions are mostly for my children, and intermingle with my dreams.

And in my dreams, I'm floating through a sea of purple dandelions while an orchestra of zebra play excerpts from the musicals of Andrew Lloyd Weber in Technicolor. What do you make of that, doctor?

The daughter's view

As I sit here, swinging on my chair and clapping along to the Jackson Five, I wonder where my ambition has gone these days. It's the long, wet summer holiday of '98 and I've got no beach to go to. No swimming to be done. No driving impulse to do anything, really. I blame the weather. Even the dog is distinctly sleepier and grumpier when the weather is black and dull.

But I'll tell you a secret: I'm gonna be bigger than Kool. I'm gonna be huge, one day soon. It'll all drop on to my knees like angel dust and I'll wake up famous. Sorry to sound arrogant, dahlings, (need to practice for interviews), but it's not a rumour. It's all true.

Fame is a natural thing: the people who are meant for it don't seem to need to reach out for it. Ringo Starr, one of my favouritest famous people at the moment, was 'not good enough' to play on the first Beatles single after he joined, but has proven his worth and joined the ranks of the toppest drummers of the whole world. Irvine Welsh didn't do publicity, photo shoots, TV, radio ... he just let his book out there, loose on the unsuspecting public. Now the rights to *Trainspotting* have made him a millionaire. If you dare to dream, then the results speak for themselves.

My ambition is more of a steadily held belief, like the golden ladder that presents itself, or the steps that collapse when you stop believing. It's not a working, driving machine: it's a God-given confidence in what I do, the people I meet, the contacts I make, the words I put on paper. It's the glasses through which I watch opportunities arrive. This is a happier, less selfish ambition than most. It is a lazy (never said I was hard-working!) ride down the path life takes me; not a future-gazing, determined climb.

My 'ambition' if it has to be called that, is not what will get me to where I'm going, because I don't know where I am going – I'm content to leave it to the silent, golden hand of God.

> 'For I know the plans I have for you,' declares the Lord, 'plans to prosper you and not to harm you, plans to give you a hope and a future.' Jeremiah 29:11

Random jottings

The mother's view

'What on earth are random jottings?' Anna asks.
  'Just what it says,' I reply.
  'Well, what am I supposed to write?'
  'Anything that comes into your mind,' I say. 'We need to fill a space in the book.'
  You can tell this book is very well planned. Anyway I have a theory to prove, but more of that later.
  So, lying in bed this morning, I noticed that a gentle tapping on my right cheek leads to a resounding booming in my left ear. Jiggling my legs has a similar effect, as does shrugging my shoulders. I think I shall compose a symphony in six parts entitled 'Ear-ly Morning Blues.'
  I had a bad day yesterday but I had only slight blues this morning. Listening to Radio 2 in bed at 9.25 a.m. (such decadence, that's what half term does to you) I became vaguely aware of the words of a song, probably called 'The best is yet to come'. Oh goody, something to look forward to. But then I think, suppose the best is not yet to come but has, in fact, actually been and gone. It reminded me of the film 'As good as it gets'. I'd assumed that 'as good as it gets' was quite a positive statement, you know, it doesn't get any better than this, this is fantastic. But Jack Nicholson uses the phrase when he asks a group of patients waiting to see their therapist, 'What if this is as good as it gets?' Puts a whole new slant on it, doesn't it?
  So it's a good thing that the speaker in church last Sunday, a highly talented teacher cum actor cum electrician offered a different perspective. Quoting some great, probably Buddhist because it sounds like the sort of thing Buddhists say, teacher, he said, 'Each thousand mile journey starts with one step.' Deep and meaningful, eh? Enjoy the journey. Alan, the speaker, said that, not me, although I'm thinking of getting it made into a poster to stick on every wall in my house.
  So, anyway, my theory. I suggest that there is no such thing as random thoughts. Each thought that enters our mind is related in some way to a thought already there, or is suggested to our brain by an external influence. With great thinkers the logical progression is easy to see; with others of us the path may be slightly harder to follow but it's there. (Robert is reading this over my shoulder. He pats me on the head and says, 'Yes Mum, whatever you say, Mum.' He's a lovely boy.)

The daughter's view

I have hiccups. Can you die from hiccups? I think probably. If you have it for a long time. It's always a worry to me, though. (Three, four, five, six, seven, eight, nine, ten, eleven.) You can die from holding your breath too (nineteen, twenty). Twenty doesn't usually work; I normally have to go further, past thirty sometimes, which means I'm even closer to dying than I was before, when I just had hiccups. Except, this time, they've gone. I can feel a little one in my throat that didn't quite finish properly, but it won't explode all on its own. I win.

Hmm. The thing with writing so-called 'random jottings' is that they might turn out to be too random and too, um, jottery. I expect Mum's are though. She's a crazy woman, you know. She hides behind the bathroom door. I am definitely expecting her jottings to be random. Probably about Sainsbury's, and I know, how they changed the layout. Wouldn't be surprised to see tinned food and porridge make an appearance either. We don't see one another's articles, you know. We just have to guess at what the other one's written. That's the original concept. It's quite fun writing in secret, but it can also get frustrating. ('How did *you* write Random J's, Mum? I can't *think*, whinge, whinge . . .')

Did you see that word back there, that I made up? It was near the start of the paragraph. Jottery. It wasn't a bad non-word, as it happens, and I'm sure you understood it. I do that a lot. It's part of my cunning scheme to take over the world by altering the English language to one of my own creation. I do it (subconsciously) all the time. Like Dylan Thomas, who made up tons of words in *Under Milkwood*. He was from Swansea too. Maybe it's something in the sea, that skewiffs our brains and wingles our words so they look sort of wonky. Approximate versions of real dictionary-words, with little hats on. Chocolate- or Verb-Dipped fritters of words. De-boringed words you see. I suppose it's not an altogether useful habit. Not terribly academic.

I am writing about nonsense again. I really should be writing wise and intellectual, thought-provoking, things. Posers. Questions of life. Answers. Philosophical debate. But there's a quote, I think from Shakespeare. You can tell I like Shakespeare can't you? There're liberal splatterings of him all over the place. (There was another one – a non-word.) Anyway. The quote is, 'So wise so young, they say, never live long.' So I should not try to be wise. Not that it's difficult. The trickiest things to write are the clever sentences. (An Insight to a Writer's Mind – in 400 words). That's enough now. You must be fed up. I'll leave it in Mum's capable hands. (She's crazier than me.)

> 'Though this be madness, there be method in it.' From *Hamlet* – Shakespeare

The sounds of music

The mother's view

Lying in bed last night listening to the quiet, I realised how familiar it was. A comfortable recognisable sort of quiet. Quite different from the night-time quiet of any other place. I pick up the noise of the occasional car or motorbike passing but the sources of the secret night-time noises that make my quiet so distinctive evade me.

Is silence attainable these days? Unless you're a monk with a four-foot-thick walled cell, it is very hard to listen to perfect silence. Is there even such a thing as silence?

Certainly not in our house.

It is not unknown for each of the children to be playing music in their rooms, while I listen to the radio in the kitchen, and the television talks to itself in the lounge. Add to that the dog barking, the telephone ringing, and the toilet door banging in the wind, and it becomes clear why we don't get many visitors.

I'm just as guilty as anyone. As soon as I go into the kitchen I tune into Radio 2 unless it's lunch time and Jimmy Young's on. Even I have my standards. Good ole Terry Wogan's my favourite. (Did I say I had standards?) At least they play some good music on Radio 2, sixties and seventies, and even the more tuneful of today's songs. That's the point of it, isn't it, a song you can sing along with? I am careful though not to inflict my singing on anyone outside of the immediate family circle. I have few enough friends as it is. Which makes a comment made to my son recently rather perplexing. He was introduced to a lady who said, 'Oh yes, I know your mother. She sings.' I can only assume that she mistook my screaming up the stairs, 'Will you all shut up!' for an operatic aria.

It's interesting seeing the children's musical tastes change as they grow. We've done New Kids on the Block, Take That, Madonna, Michael Jackson, Oasis. Now it's the serious stuff. I can tell because the names of the bands are becoming more obscure, and the noise they make even more unfathomable. The Beatles are the exception. They persist as the sole musical link between Anna and me.

When I'm concentrating, like now, I need something less distracting than Stevie Wonder's Superstition *or Scaffold's* Lily the Pink. *That's where my Gregorian chants come in. You know where you are with a Gregorian chant.*

The daughter's view

'Desert Island Discs' (sorry, couldn't resist): I'll have to choose *Hakuna Matata*, y'know, the one that's on the Disney film *The Lion King*, which I listen to when I write, a lot. Couldn't live without it, Sue. I just like it 'cause it's the happiest, most feel-good song in the world, and it's from a musical, and I know all the words. 'And oh, the shame! Thought of changing my name! And got downhearted, every time that I ... (Hey, Pumbaa, not in front of the kids.)'

What is really interesting about anyone is what they don't like, what gets on their nerves, what they'd die to avoid – not the music they enjoy. People who say: 'I like everything really' immediately alert you of their intense dullness. Someone without the passion to really hate a piece of music is not someone worth bothering to waste sweet voice tones on. You may well like listening to lots of different kinds of music (these days the range makes it impossible not to – every song defines a different species – speed garage, jazz funk, glam rock, fusion punk, and any other two words you fancy stringing together), but don't say you like everything, please. As far as I'm concerned, the more obscure your taste, the better. 'Everything' includes – what? – the theme tune to *Blind Date*? Chopsticks? Peter Andre? Purleeaase. The most interesting music fan is to be found scavenging for rare seventies flops and out-of-print Disney singles at the back of a second-hand record store. On vinyl.

Of course vinyl hasn't gone out yet. New DJs without the technology still learn on record decks. I had a bash this week, on my brother's set of borrowed equipment, and although it's addictive, I think it's hallucinatory: while be-headphoned and pulling knobs behind a deck, you forget to step back and actually listen to the sound. About all I can do that's listenable-to is add bits off the Muppet Show album to today's more artistically mixed tunes. 'Well, Fonzy, I'm afraid it doesn't quite make it on a record.' Or James Brown: 'Fellas I'm ready to do get up and do my thing!! Like a sex machine! Movin'! An' groovin'!!'

I'm always delighted to be able to reveal my pet hates of the music world. I do have a wide appreciation and open mind towards anything that has a sound, but I will not say that I like everything. I hate, hate, hate, Gregorian chants (thankfully that was just a phase of my mother's – I hope) and I also hate, hate, hate Radios 2 and 4. OK. So Radio 4 doesn't play any music, but I still hate it. And Radio 2 – hello? – is purely croaky old fogey stuff, plus Terry Wogan and his TOG business, you see it's not just the music. It's being force-fed it that I object to, I suppose. I haven't willingly subjected my ears to the station, and I hope I never will. I don't believe in torturing one's children. Dishwashing rotas are quite enough of a punishment for growing out of shoes too quickly.

> **Have a bop around with God;**
> **dance around to the music God plays for you.**
> **Twirl and swirl with him all over the world;**
> **in the highest places and the quietest bring his noise,**
> **sing with God to the sounds of bagpipes, banjos and bass guitar;**
> **for he is the Creator, the Dancer, the Singer and the greatest Swinger.**
> An All-New Psalm, by Anna.

Boyfriends

The mother's view

Dear Claire,
At what age should girls start dating?
Yours anxiously, Confused of Tunbridge Wells.

Perhaps the fact that I was a late starter has coloured my view on this matter. Thirteen-year-olds holding hands and 'going out' is not something I can take seriously, although I realise that some are deadly, and regrettably, serious. I suppose with your own children, it's even harder because they still seem so young, so child-like in many ways. Still, even someone as 'away with the fairies' as me can't help but notice that relationships do happen and are yearned after. When Anna was fifteen or so I worried that she would be left out if all her friends found boyfriends and she didn't, and I also worried that if she did have a boyfriend her school work would suffer. Let's face it, I was going to worry whatever happened.

So, anyway, she met a boy, and, yes, her school work did suffer. More than that, the whole foundation of her life was shaken. Thankfully she was held together, and restored, by God who sees and takes seriously the pain of teenage broken hearts.

After that names came and went; phone calls came or didn't; and the question arose: at what age should boys start dating?

I am seriously concerned that Robert will end up marrying some scheming hussy (see, I've got all the terminology ready to be a mother-in-law who thinks no-one's good enough for her baby) who's got her claws into him, simply because he's too kind-hearted to say no.

On the other hand, my friend seems dead set on getting her son matched up as soon as possible, helping him along the way by sending Valentine cards on his behalf and offering him money to take out a suitable female. At least I don't interfere that much!?

Anna meanwhile is happily dating a lovely boy who is kind to children and looks after her. What more can I ask?

The daughter's view

I hate seeing couples. Even when I'm in one, I still hate them. Just seeing them. You just know that they're a hundred times happier and more perfect than you, and that he buys her flowers and she rubs his feet every night. They have shnooky names for each other and cuddle (eeeewww). You know that they never fight, they never cry, they're never apart, just glued together like double-sided sticky tape. They have meals with other Perfect Couples and act grown-up, or they go to dinner-parties and act grown-up, and they go out to posh restaurants for anniversaries where the waiters recognise them and ask about their cat. They've probably all got cats too, like Ross in *Friends*, a shared one if they don't live together, which is guaranteed to last for ever, just like them and their hand-holding.

Of course, I also hate seeing single women, because they are obviously all a thousand times more beautiful than you, with much more chance of achieving PerfectCoupledom, and they wear high-heels. Leather, PVC, short or low things. Hairdressed hair. You know who they are. They'll never get wrinkles. You've just got no chance.

They don't have these peculiar habits that make you a nightmare for boyfriends, that nobody else on earth has. Habits like not brushing your teeth as soon as you get up and then forgetting all day, or writing poems about the Pink Panther, or having photos of yourself down-the-toilet around the house, or talking about your obsession with ears. Sound familiar? Ah, then you understand. I knew somebody would.

I've often thought, as one by one these little oddities come out, that I should wear a placard or write on my forehead: WEIRDO – BEWARE when I'm single. A kind of pre-warning, so people know what they're heading for. Other people could have: COMMITMENT PROBLEM (wouldn't that be a useful one?), or ONE NIGHT STANDER or SETTLING DOWN. These would make life so much easier, but the thing is, if I did ever get myself a man (who'd choose a FREAK over a DRUG ADDICT?), he'd probably be seriously strange. Who wants to go out with a crazee?

But as it is, the poor victims get to discover the WEIRDO beneath the mask on their own. I try to break them in gently ... I suppose we all do in our own little ways. My long-term Patient-and-Responsible-type boyfriend waited a couple of months before farting out loud in confined spaces, in my presence. That was a treat, and joyfully discovered. I just hope he hasn't got any more placard signs to come out of the drawer (or, more importantly, his drawers).

> Dear God,
> It's hard to stay focused on you sometimes with all this young love confusion.
>> *So is this it then, God? The One, at least for the moment?*
> Bless me in my relationship(s) and don't let me lose hold of you whatever I do.
>> *Will it last? Will it hurt? Will it grow?*
> Bless Mum and Dad's relationship too ... I forget that they were in love once ...
>> *Will she abandon you, or me?*
> ... and that you see they still are. Bless and strengthen them as they grow old and crochety!
>> *Keep speaking into her life, Lord; keep the love lines open.*
>> *Amen.*

The big sleep

The mother's view

I shouldn't be trying to write this now, I'm feeling irritable and it will show in what I write. But then again, it's probably best to write it now, get my feelings down while I feel them. It's quarter to twelve, nearly lunchtime, and Anna has just emerged from bed. That's half a day she has wasted. Some of us have done, well, half a day's work, already. And what's the first thing she does when she gets up, apart from eat and watch daytime trashyvision? Phone her friend. 'Sorry did I wake you?' Did you wake her? Such concern is touching. Pity you didn't worry about waking me when you came to bed at midnight. And that was an early night.

'There, there, mother, have a cup of tea, you'll soon feel better.' She would put the kettle on and make me one but she has to shower and dress and do her hair and her make-up and her eyes. So I make myself a cup of tea, and wonder why I'm so ineffectual as a mother, a bossy mother at least. If I had my act together, I'd have these three children up and dressed by nine, and then start them on their chores for the day: doing dishes, ironing, cleaning, running errands, gardening, walking the dog, and bringing me cups of tea at regular intervals.

Don't get me wrong, it's not her sleeping I have a problem with – I'm very fond of bed myself – I just wish she'd do it at more civilised hours. She can cope with turning night into day. She doesn't have to get up at the same early hour whatever time she gets to sleep. Whereas some of us . . .

I'm beginning to sound like an old hag. Just because lack of sleep has resulted in me looking like one doesn't mean I have to sound like one as well.

Mike has a habit of reminding me of our courting days. Every Saturday morning he would get up, visit the supermarket, do his weekly shop, take it home and unpack and store the food, before driving the ten miles to come and see me, bearing his gift of a cream cake. Inevitably I'd still be curled up in bed when he arrived.

I'm torn now on how to end this. Will it be 'Like mother, like daughter' or 'Oh, happy days'?

The daughter's view

'Rob.'

'Mmm?'

'Tell me what to write about sleep.'

'You should know, Anna.'

'Oh, Ro-ob!'

'Oh wow! Look at that bird! It's got a stone in its mouth! Oh my gosh! It's eating a stone! Did you know that jays are too fat to stand on branches. Oh my gosh! It's picking up another one! Fat pie!'

'Come on, stop avoiding the question.'

'What do you want me to say?'

'Something interesting.'

'Something deep and philosophical. Sleep. Hang on. I'm trying to think of something to make me sound brainy. Oh — I've got it. If I sleep well, it is because I sleep on the beds of giants.'

'You made that up didn't you.'

'It's from something Galileo said. I've altered it slightly. I've got another good one too. Opium is the religion of the masses.'

'If I sleep well, it's just a phase. I'm an insomniac.'

'Really?'

'No, not really, I'm just trying to sound interesting.'

'Shall I tell you about the dream where I was being chased by dwarfs through the underground train system in West Cross?'

'Go on then.'

'I was being chased, by a — you know what a Morph is?'

'I thought you said a dwarf.'

'No, a Morph. You know those little plasticine people on that art programme.'

'So what were the origins of that?'

'I dunno. I just dreamt it.'

'You can normally trace dreams to something that happened in your day. Well, I can, anyway. Dad? Have you had any weird dreams?'

'I dreamed I was a spy the other day.'

'That's what happens when you play "Gangsters" on the computer too much. Doesn't that tell you something? Neil. Have you had any weird dreams recently?'

'Of course not.'

'That doesn't surprise me. Neil's got problems,' Robert whispers.

'Neil, you must have had one weird dream in your life.'

'Anna, he's just generally weird all the time. It's his everyday life. Neil gets chased by Morphs in school and stuff.'

'Neil, just think of a dream. And tell me.'

'Robert got shot.'

'And?'

'That's it.'

'He just made that up off the top of his head.'

'That's a fantasy isn't it, not a dream. I know. Neil wriggles in his sleep.'

'I think I know that. Squeak squeak squeak!' (Robert does a loud impression of Neil's bed)

'Any more contributions to make?'

'Vegetarians really annoy me.'

'Thanks. Why?'

'They eat vegetables. Not meat. Vegetables are horrible. Meat's nice.'

'No it's not, meat's horrible.'

'It's lovely.'

THE END

'I will lie down and sleep in peace, for you alone, O Lord, make me dwell in safety.' Psalm 4:8